THE GENERAL EPISTLE OF JAMES

A DEVOTIONAL COMMENTARY
Edited by the Rev. A. R. BUCKLAND, M.A.

THE GENERAL EPISTLE OF
JAMES

A DEVOTIONAL COMMENTARY

By the

Rev. CHARLES BROWN
Author of 'Light and Life,' etc.

WIPF & STOCK · Eugene, Oregon

Wipf and Stock Publishers
199 W 8th Ave, Suite 3
Eugene, OR 97401

The General Epistle of James
A Devotional Commentary
By Brown, Charles and Buckland, A. R.
Softcover ISBN-13: 978-1-6667-0592-8
Hardcover ISBN-13: 978-1-6667-0593-5
eBook ISBN-13: 978-1-6667-0594-2
Publication date 3/10/2021
Previously published by The Union Press, 1907

This edition is a scanned facsimile
of the original edition published in 1907.

CONTENTS

PAGE

I.
THE WRITER.   9
James i. 1.

II.
TRIALS AND TEMPTATIONS   .   .   . 13
James i. 2-8.

III.
THE TRIAL AND THE REFUGE   .   .   . 21
James i. 9-18.

IV.
NOT DECEIVED—AS TO GOD   .   .   . 26
James i. 16-18.

V.
NOT DECEIVED—AS TO OURSELVES   .   . 33
James i. 19-21.

VI.
NOT DECEIVED—AS TO THE BIBLE   .   . 38
James i. 22-25.

Contents

VII.

NOT DECEIVED—ABOUT RELIGION   .   .   41

James i. 26, 27.

VIII.

RESPECT OF PERSONS   44

James ii. 1-13.

IX.

FAITH AND WORKS   55

James ii. 14-26.

X.

ON SPEECH   .   .   .   .   ,   59

James iii. 1, 2.

XI.

ON THE TEACHER   62

James iii. 1, 2.

XII.

THE CONTROL OF THE TONGUE .   .   .   66

James iii. 3-8.

XIII.

POSSIBILITIES OF EVIL AND BLESSING .   .   72

James iii. 9-12.

Contents

XIV.

WISDOM, TRUE AND FALSE . . . 76

James iii. 13-16.

XV.

DIVINE WISDOM 81

James iii. 17.

XVI.

THE THIRST FOR PLEASURE . . . 84

James iii. 18; iv. 1-4.

XVII.

FRIEND OF THE WORLD, OR OF GOD . . 88

James iv. 4-6.

XVIII.

HUMBLE SUBMISSION TO GOD . . . 92

James iv. 6-10.

XIX.

A DANGER AND A REMEDY . . . 97

James iv. 11, 12.

XX.

PLANNING WITHOUT GOD 101

James iv. 13, 14.

Contents

PAGE

XXI.

IF THE LORD WILL 104

James iv. 15-17.

XXII.

GREEDY RICH AND SUFFERING POOR . 107

James v. 1-6.

XXIII.

A PLEA FOR PATIENCE 115

James v. 7-12.

XXIV.

PRAYER AND MEANS 122

James v. 13-15.

XXV.

THE MINISTRY OF RESTORATION . . . 130

James v. 16-20.

I

THE WRITER

JAMES i. 1.

JAMES, a servant of God and of the Lord Jesus Christ.

THIS is a letter written primarily to Jews.
Throughout all the countries mentioned in Acts
ii. 9-11, Jews were scattered, and it was to Jews
everywhere, and to Christian Jews in particular,
that this letter was sent. There is a good deal
that is distinctively Jewish in its style and spirit.
Indeed, in many of its parts it reminds us rather
of the Old Testament than of the New. We
might imagine in places that we were reading
one of the old prophets. There seems to be no
reasonable doubt that it was written by the
brother of our Lord. He bore an ancient name.
We call it 'James,' for so it has come to us
through the metamorphosis of several languages.
But the countrymen of the writer called him by
the name of the patriarch Jacob, one of the
commonest of names in a nation which was poor
in names.

James i. 1.
The Author.

9

The General Epistle of James

James i. 1.
The Three Jameses.
There are at least three Jameses mentioned in the New Testament. (1) The son of Zebedee, (2) the son of Alphæus or James-the-Less, (3) the brother of our Lord. Of the first we know that he was the proto-martyr among the Apostles. Fourteen years after the ascension of our Lord, before he had had an opportunity to impress himself upon the world, we read (Acts xii. 2) that Herod killed James the brother of John with the sword. Of the second, we know nothing. He seems to have come to no position and no influence. Of the third, we may note that he is mentioned in the very chapter which tells of the martyrdom of his namesake, and mentioned in such a way as to imply that he had reached a place of authority, or at least of importance, in the Church at Jerusalem (Acts xii. 17). How that came to be we are not told.

The Brethren of the Lord.
The first mention made of James, the brother of our Lord, is in Matt. xiii. 55, where the people of Nazareth call in question the authority of our Lord, and find offence in Him because they know His relatives, who are their neighbours. Then the writer of the fourth Gospel tells us that even the brethren of Jesus did not believe on Him (John vii. 5).

Into the suggestions that 'the brethren' of our Lord were not, after all, His brothers as

10

The Writer

we understand the word, I need not go. There seems to be no reason whatever why the term brethren should be taken to mean anything else than what we should mean by the use of the term brother. It is explicit enough, and if other relatives were intended it seems reasonable to conclude that another term would have been used. *James i. 1.*

How the brothers of the Lord were turned from unbelief to faith we are not told. But we learn from St Paul (1 Cor. xv. 7) that our Lord appeared to James after His resurrection; and we may be permitted to think that either the closing events in the life of our Lord or His death itself, or perhaps this appearance to James— one or other or all of them provided the means of bringing him to believe in his Divine Kinsman.

Be that as it may, we find that among the company of the disciples waiting in Jerusalem and praying for the fulfilment of the promise, are Mary the mother of Jesus and His brethren. So that James was among those who received the Holy Ghost at Pentecost. By the time of St Paul's conversion he seems to have come to some position of authority in the Church at Jerusalem (Gal. i. 19). And when the Apostles and elders met to consider on what terms Gentiles should be admitted to the Church, James was the presiding elder. There are many similarities *James, the Lord's Brother.*

11

The General Epistle of James

James i. 1. between the speech then delivered (Acts xv. 14) and the letter which is before us now, as any reader even of the English version may see.

It is not necessary to enter here into a discussion of the grounds for or against the conclusion that the letter before us was written by James, the brother of our Lord. I accept the arguments in favour of his authorship.

The Lord's Brother and the Christology of this Epistle. But the question may arise : 'If this be so, how is it that there is no claim to the fact in the letter itself, and that indeed so little is said about our Lord in its pages ?' I have no theory to uphold. I would only suggest for one thing the possibility of James not wishing to presume upon his relation to the Lord, and for the other I would point out what will be discovered as we proceed—that the letter is full of echoes of the teaching of Christ, that James calls himself His 'bondslave,' and Him 'the Lord of Glory.' This is the man doubtless whose letter is before us— a man brought up in the same home as Jesus, who had come by the power of the Holy Spirit to see His greatness, and to a position of great influence in His Church. He writes to people passing through a time of fierce trial, and who are beset by temptations. We shall see what he says.

II

TRIALS AND TEMPTATIONS

JAMES i. 1-8.

JAMES, a servant of God and of the Lord Jesus Christ, to the twelve tribes which are of the Dispersion, greeting. Count it all joy, my brethren, when ye fall into manifold temptations; knowing that the proof of your faith worketh patience. And let patience have *its* perfect work, that ye may be perfect and entire, lacking in nothing. But if any of you lacketh wisdom, let him ask of God, who giveth to all liberally and upbraideth not; and it shall be given him. But let him ask in faith, nothing doubting: for he that doubteth is like the surge of the sea driven by the wind and tossed. For let not that man think that he shall receive anything of the Lord; a double-minded man, unstable in all his ways.

You will observe that the first lesson of this Epistle is one upon Trials and Temptations. A very familiar topic for Christians of all ages, and a subject which should commend this letter to us. There is no congregation of people gathered anywhere for public worship in which there are not those who are tried and tempted. There are few things more necessary than that we should have right conceptions of the great subject, and

James i. 1-8.
A Familiar Theme.

13

The General Epistle of James

James i. 1-8.

that we should regard it from a right point of view.

Temptation and Joy.

You will observe, if I may put it in this way, that James *has no pity for us*; that does not mean that he does not appreciate the difficulties of the position of people who are tried, but that they really are not to be pitied. He rebukes afterwards the people who have no compassion for the needs of their fellows; yet he does not consider that the Christian who falls into divers trials because he *is* a Christian is to be compassionated, but rather to be envied. So he challenges our attention at the very outset of his letter, and drives us to think by paradoxical teaching. '*Count it all joy when ye fall into divers trials.*' He has said 'All joy' to you in his greeting. Here is the ground for joy.

A Message, not of Nature, but Grace.

This runs clear against the bent and tendency of human nature. We count it all joy when we escape from danger or sorrow or loss. We think of some friend who has a sick wife, an afflicted child, or particular trouble in his business—and we thank God that we have been preserved. It is just possible—according to James—that they are to be envied and we to be pitied. And you know that he is not alone in this kind of teaching. Paul is with him, and Peter, and the Master

14

Trials and Temptations

whom he remembers so well. Indeed, this is an echo of the Divine teaching: 'Blessed are ye, when men shall revile you, and persecute you, and say all manner of evil against you. Rejoice, and be exceeding glad.' ^{James i. 1-8.}

Still, it is a hard saying, and we cannot pretend to understand it until we get on *to his next word,* in which it clearly appears that it is not the trial itself, but its purpose, that is to cause us thanksgiving and joy. What is going on, according to James, while trial is being applied? Through this circumstance God is touching the soul; purifying, cleansing, shaping, developing qualities in the man that could be developed in no other way. Through the afflicted child, wife, husband; through the fierce trial in business—resourcefulness, patience, power to endure, courage, modesty, sympathy, are being developed. While you are pitying, God is using these agents for the cleansing, enriching, upbuilding of *character*; and there is nothing so precious in God's sight as character. ^{A Hard Saying made Clear.}

Therefore, 'count it all joy,' 'knowing that the proof of your faith worketh patience'—we get an echo of Paul's word here: 'Tribulation worketh patience.' '*But let patience have her perfect work,*' or, if you like, let the power to endure be made perfect, and it can only be ^{Trial, Patience, and Impatience.}

15

The General Epistle of James

James i. 1-8.

made perfect by enduring. God is fashioning a beautiful thing in your life by trial. Do not shatter this thing to pieces by breaking out and breaking down just at the crucial point.

It is quite possible, as we know too well, that the trying of faith may work impatience. Even eminent men, and men who are supposed to be great, may manifest much impatience, and some amount of bad temper, when they are resisted and crossed. When they do it, or we, who are not eminent, do that; when we resent criticism and are angry with people who point out faults; when ill-will and revenge are cherished towards those who wrong us—then we are resisting a discipline which might be most wholesome for character and spirit. That discipline may be just what we need for the humbling of pride, the rebuking of selfishness, and the refinement of some part of our nature. James, the brother of the Lord, was no stranger to trial. He is not mocking us in such a word as this. He is repeating to us the burden of the whole of the New Testament. May God help every tried heart to receive it. *Trial*, even manifold trial—people who trouble and cross, circumstances that vex and harass—may be necessary to the upbuilding and development of character.

Trial and Character.

Here is the purpose of trial; it is as necessary

16

Trials and Temptations

as any other element in order to secure the result of verse 4: '*That ye may be full grown and mature, lacking in nothing.*' Do you never sigh and long for a fully-developed character? Are we so far gone in seeking gain and ease and pleasure that we have no deep passionate longing to be like Christ, to grow up into Him in all things? It has never been accomplished without trial, and never will be. Blessed is the man—unspeakably blessed—who, by whatever means, is being conformed to the image of Christ Jesus. *James i. 1-8.*

You will observe by verses 5-8 the connection between trial and prayer. We are not to lay too great stress upon the little word with which verse 5 starts in the Authorised Version, as though James were conveying a delicate and ironical suggestion that a man might possibly lack wisdom. He takes it for granted that men *do* lack it. And if we take the term 'wisdom' in its lowest interpretation, we may fairly say that it is especially *difficult to be wise in time of trial,* to behave wisely when you are wronged and insulted. 'Goaded beyond endurance,' as you say, irritated by unjust treatment, treated without consideration or justice; misunderstood, misjudged, annoyed, bullied—it is very difficult to keep a clear and sound judgment, and most of *Trial and Wisdom.*

The General Epistle of James

James i.
1-8.

all a Christian temper then. When men are exasperated they are apt to do unwise things. I am very much impressed with what I read in 1 Sam. xviii. 14 and 15, after the capricious and evil-minded king had attempted the life of David: 'And David behaved himself wisely in all his ways, and when Saul saw that, he stood in awe of him.' Wise behaviour under trial may take long to tell, but it does tell. It seems less effective than some dramatic and foolish *outbreak*; it certainly is less sensational, but it is really more efficacious.

Wisdom
and Folly.

But when James speaks of wisdom he means that large and sagacious view of life which sees all things, even trial, in their true perspective and colouring—the quality which is opposed to *folly*, that great characteristic of human nature. And we need it in other matters than in trial. In the training of children, as to their tastes, habits, conception of work, etc., how often our folly, want of foresight or insight, lands us in our worst difficulties and trials. How often you see people steering straight for the rocks, and you long to avert disaster from them. Now see what James

Wisdom
and Prayer.

says: 'Let him who lacks wisdom *pray*.' A fool may become wise by waiting on God. There is such a possibility in human life as divine illumination—an enlightened and instructed consideration

Trials and Temptations

and judgment. 'If any man lack . . . let him ask . . . *and it shall be given.*' Here is another echo of the Divine Teacher's words: 'Ask, and it shall be given you.' But this passage is an enlargement of the divine teaching on the question of God's giving: 'He giveth liberally and without upbraiding,' without telling you that you deserve all the trouble into which your wilful folly had led you, and that you do not deserve the gift; 'He giveth, He upbraideth not'; for there is a way of giving that humiliates the receiver and makes him hate the giver.

James i. 1-8.

But there is also something about asking. Let him ask in faith; if you like, in *good faith*—in single *earnestness* wanting to know, that he may do the will of God; nothing *doubting* or *wavering,* or *debating,* or being *double-minded,* wanting partly your own and partly God's way; not saying: 'If the light points in that direction I shall follow it; if not, I shall not.'

Asking, Believing, Trusting.

The man who prays so as to receive, must know what he means, and mean what he says. Let a man cry with all his heart, 'Lord, what wilt Thou have me to do?' and he will not walk in darkness. The great mischief is that there is so little meaning in our prayers, so little good faith,

19

The General Epistle of James

**James i.
1-8.**
so little singleness and passionate earnestness;
where these are, wisdom will not be lacking.
Let the man who is in trial pray. 'Trust in the
Lord with all thine heart, and lean not unto thine
own understanding.'

III

THE TRIAL AND THE REFUGE

JAMES i. 9-18.

BUT let the brother of low degree glory in his high estate:
and the rich, in that he is made low: because as the flower of
the grass he shall pass away. For the sun ariseth with the
scorching wind, and withereth the grass; and the flower
thereof falleth, and the grace of the fashion of it perisheth:
so also shall the rich man fade away in his goings. Blessed
is the man that endureth temptation: for when he hath been
approved, he shall receive the crown of life, which *the Lord*
promised to them that love Him. Let no man say when he is
tempted, I am tempted of God: for God cannot be tempted
with evil, and He Himself tempteth no man: but each man
is tempted, when he is drawn away by his own lust, and
enticed. Then the lust, when it hath conceived, beareth sin:
and the sin, when it is full-grown, bringeth forth death. Be
not deceived, my beloved brethren. Every good gift and every
perfect boon is from above, coming down from the Father of
lights, with whom can be no variation, neither shadow that
is cast by turning. Of His own will He brought us forth by
the word of truth, that we should be a kind of firstfruits of His
creatures.

HERE is a very difficult passage (vers. 9-11), in **James i.**
which James shows his characteristic disregard **9-18.**
of, and almost contempt for, wealth. It is quite Temptation
and Wealth.
evident from this and other passages that there

21

The General Epistle of James

James i. 9-18. were rich people in the early Christian assemblies. And it may be—it is even probable in the light of chapter ii. 2—that there was a disposition among Christian people to exaggerate the importance of the rich man, to make too much of him, either for his own good or the good of the Church.

And here is a man who has always been poor, a working carpenter's son, who has never known luxuries, and who has the same contempt for them which Amos had—whom he very much resembles—and to whom, moreover, the perils of wealth are very obvious. Now he speaks to both poor and rich. To the first he says, Glory in your high estate, your spiritual wealth. To the other, Rejoice when you are brought low. Perhaps he means that the rich Christian was a special prize for the persecutors and spoilers of Christians—one of the trials was the loss of money ; or possibly that by the teaching of the Gospel the rich man was reduced to the level of the poor, and made to kneel by his side. Certainly he means that whatever wealth a rich man has, the day will come when he must be severed from it. The rich man as a rich man fades away, the Christian as a Christian never fades. Not by reason of riches, but by reason of God's mercy and faith, a Christian goes to live for ever with God.

The Trial and the Refuge

In the next and last paragraph, the great and important subject of temptation, as distinct from trial—temptation to evil—is treated; and it is so important as to deserve a chapter all to itself. He starts by declaring the blessedness of the man that *endureth* temptation. Not, observe, the man who *escapes* it, nor the man who is tempted, but the man who *endures*, that is, survives and conquers. It is not of necessity a blessed thing to be tempted, nor is it a blessed thing to suffer. But there is a possible blessing in it, the highest blessing that a man can win— the crown of life.

He makes a declaration which we should cling to, though we are not able to explain it.

God does not tempt men; let no man say, when the solicitation to evil is strong and fierce, 'That is God.' He cannot tempt men to evil. *And it is His will that you should conquer.* That in itself should be the earnest and the guarantee of victory. James does not mention the tempter here. He does in chapter iv. 7. He says temptation is to be traced to our desires or *lusts.* Two things are necessary to constitute temptation, namely, desire and opportunity. Often there is the third, viz. solicitation, the urging to satisfy the desire at all costs by the tempter. But, let us mark it—desire, opportunity, solicitation, all put

James i. 9-18. Temptation and Endurance.

Temptation: Its Force.

23

The General Epistle of James

James i. 9-18. together, do not constitute sin. It is when the desire breaks through the bounds of control—is yielded to, embraces the opportunity—that the deadly offspring of sin is brought forth, and it in turn bears the awful fruit of death.

You cannot read this passage without feeling the solemnity, the awful solemnity, of temptation; the times of crisis through which the soul must pass; what tragic issues depend on it.

The Conflict and the Soul. We shall be tempted, some of us, to-morrow; we shall not come out of the temptation the same people as before it came upon us, we shall perforce be either better or worse. Think of it! There is a man on whom there comes a strong, an almost burning desire, for money, say, or for some pleasure. The opportunity for gratifying the desire suddenly appears. It would be wrong, he knows; but there would be advantage in it— gain, excitement, a certain kind of intense satisfaction. Then for the time, it may be moments, hours, sometimes days, his soul is a battle-ground where fiercest conflict rages. If there is one thing which God and the angels watch with keenest interest, it is that conflict. If a man conquer, he is for ever a stronger, wiser, richer man. If he fail, if his will capitulate to his desire, he is unspeakably worse; sin has been born afresh in his nature, has come to stay.

The Trial and the Refuge

What is a man's comfort, his safeguard, in that perilous hour? His comfort—oh that he may grasp it, and grasp it close!—is that God is near and is watching. His safeguard is prayer. What does he lack? Wisdom; light to see the tragic issues that depend upon his act now ; and strength. If any man *lack* let him *ask*, and it shall be given. John Bunyan tells us that when Christian was passing through the valley of the shadow of death—which is simply a description of the most horrible temptations that a human soul can pass through—crowded with demons and hobgoblins of the pit, he came to one point where the weapon with which he had conquered Apollyon failed — even the Bible proved ineffective. There were things that cared not for it, and he was forced to betake himself to another weapon called 'All prayer.' 'So he cried in my hearing,' says Bunyan, ' O Lord, I beseech Thee, deliver my soul.' And that is a weapon which every tempted soul may use. And he who uses it may say of the dread hour of dark temptation : 'Though I walk through the valley of the shadow of death I will fear no evil, for Thou art with me.' He has learnt the great and all-sufficient lesson of trusting in God, and in that trust lies the secret of perpetual victory.

James i. 9-18. Our Refuge and Strength.

IV

NOT DECEIVED—AS TO GOD

James i. 16-18.

Be not deceived, my beloved brethren. Every good gift and every perfect boon is from above, coming down from the Father of lights, with whom can be no variation, neither shadow that is cast by turning. Of His own will He brought us forth by the word of truth, that we should be a kind of firstfruits of His creatures.

James i. 16-18. 'Beloved'

The keynote of the passage before us is in the verse with which we start: 'Be not deceived.' We see with what loving urgency the exhortation is pressed upon the attention of the readers. 'Beloved brethren' has become a hackneyed pulpit phrase with us, and a man may use it without having any love in his heart for those he addresses; but as James uses it—and he uses it often, as will be seen in our journey through this letter—it is an expression of a deep and warm affection, a most loving solicitude for those to whom he writes. And his placing of the appeal on this loving basis shows at once the importance of the subject and his deep desire that the appeal should go home to their hearts.

Not Deceived—As to God

You will see, if you will look, that in different forms this word occurs three times in this chapter— *James i. 16-18. 'Be not Deceived.'*

Verse 16—'Be not deceived,' do not allow yourselves to be misled by others.

Verse 22 opens another possibility to us: we may *delude our own selves*, we may throw dust into our own eyes. By bad logic, bad reasoning, we may trick ourselves into wrong.

Verse 26—A man may deceive his own heart, may lead it astray from the high road of truth and holiness, mislead and misplace his affection and sympathy, so that they shall be bestowed on altogether wrong things. Three different words are used in these three passages for the same thing, and are in accord with the rest of the teaching of the New Testament, to the effect that one of the greatest dangers of the heart of man is that of *being deceived*. The heart is deceitful above all things, and is itself capable of being deceived. There are matters before us concerning which we may be deceived, and they are the greatest matters that can occupy our thoughts. In the first place—

We may be deceived concerning God. *There* is the root of so much wrong-doing and wrong-thinking. Concerning His nature we may be deceived, and concerning the things that come *Deceived about God.*

27

The General Epistle of James

James i. 16-18. from Him. It needs absolutely no argument to make us realise that our life is largely governed and coloured by our conception of God, and that both by our own predilections and by the teachings and guessings of men we may be deceived.

What grotesque, what hideous, what foolish images of God have been fashioned by the mind and thought, and worshipped by men in all ages! And what absurd and wicked and cruel actions have flowed from such conceptions. 'Be not deceived,' cries Paul, 'God is not mocked.' He is not such a being as can be befooled by the tricks and subterfuges and pretences of men.

God's Gifts. Here is the spacious and soul-resting conception of God which James brings to us—would that we could write it on our hearts! God is good, only and changelessly good, and nothing but good comes from .His hand. He does not tempt men to evil—that is not the kind of giving that proceeds from Him, but all good giving and all perfect boons. The thing which you acquire through your own labour—and the thing that you have done nothing to earn; everything that is continuous, like daily strength and daily bread, and everything that is complete in itself, like a little child, is God's gift. All human love and friendship, all good laws and customs, all temporal

Not Deceived—As to God

mercies, all that enriches character, 'cometh down from above.' James i. 16-18.

You and I would have a sheet-anchor in all the storms of life, if we could only cling to the doctrine of James here—which is the doctrine of the whole Bible—viz. that *God is good*; that the Judge of the whole earth must do right; if we could say with Whittier :— God's Goodness.

> 'Yet in the maddening maze of things,
>   And tossed by storm and flood,
> To one fixed trust my spirit clings—
>   I know that God is good.'

How do I know it? 'He that spared not His own Son, but delivered Him up for us all, how shall He not also with Him freely give us all things?' (Rom. viii. 32).

There follows a positive statement concerning God which is most important. *'He is the Father of lights.'* James is a wonderful man for metaphors; and here he seems to be taking his readers out into the open air and bidding them look up at the sun, and think of God as the Creator of it and its light. He thinks of the sun as the source of all light and life, and God created the sun. But the sun is all inadequate to express the idea of God, there is no *parallax*, no change of position in Him, and He casts no shadow. God the Father of Lights.

29

The General Epistle of James

James i. 16-18.

God is light, and in Him is no darkness at all. James is arguing, if I may say so, for the absolute trustworthiness of God.

Many Lights from One God.

But we have a right to use this figure in a very wide and manifold way, and to say, that of all light that shines among men, God is the author. The light of reason, intellect, humour, the light of comfort and love that shines out from human hearts in the hour of sorrow, is from God. The light that shines on your perplexity in business, showing you clearly the way out, may come from a shrewd man of business; but it may be as truly divine guidance as though it shone into your heart direct from the Bible. The gas-light that illumines our buildings comes from the sun; it has been hidden for ages in the coal of the primeval forests, and needs labour to extract it; but there is no doubt about its origin. So light may break out even from some pagan philosophy, and my soul may hail it as the light of truth; and I know that all truth, wheresoever found, comes from God, and that He has in all ages been seeking to illumine the minds of men.

Access to the Light.

I personally find in this a strong hidden argument for prayer. 'God is the Father of lights.' *I may have access to Him at all seasons.* I need never therefore remain in the darkness—I have a sure word of prophecy which is as a light

30

Not Deceived—As to God

shining in a dark place—and here it is;—'He that followeth *Me* shall not walk in darkness, but shall have the light of life.' **James i. 16-18.**

It is very interesting to observe the quarter to which James looks for proof of the doctrine of God's pure goodness on which he is insisting. It is not to absence of trial and temptation, nor even to deliverance from trial and temptation; not to outward things at all; but to *regeneration*, spiritual renewal (ver. 18). That he declares is the work of God, and it is all of His sovereign will. **Regeneration of God's Sovereign Grace.**

It is a somewhat unusual line of evidence to go upon, so far as I know. Your spiritual life is a great fact, a blessed fact; consciousness of forgiveness, assurance of God's love and favour, hope of eternal blessedness is in it, and of that life God is the author. Into its spacious privileges He has led you. 'Of His own will,' (what can that will be but goodwill?) and He can never go back from that, for there is no variation in Him. All the blessed inheritance of the redeemed is God's will for you, the work of His electing and prevenient grace. And if we ask '*why*,' as related to others, this grace has come to you, the answer of James is, 'That you might be a kind of firstfruits,'—a sample of what God wills to do for all men. His purposes are universal;

The General Epistle of James

**James i.
16-18.**

we are simply the first sheaves from the great harvest-field of the world.

So with these words of clear declaration he seeks to deliver them from delusion concerning God.

V

NOT DECEIVED—AS TO OURSELVES

James i. 19-21

YE know *this*, my beloved brethren. But let every man be swift to hear, slow to speak, slow to wrath: for the wrath of man worketh not the righteousness of God. Wherefore putting away all filthiness and overflowing of wickedness, receive with meekness the implanted word, which is able to save your souls.

WE are not to be deceived about *ourselves.* Here is the possibility of another fatal mistake on the other side. A man may have such an idea of the goodness and good will of God that he may imagine all will be well with him, however he lives. He may fall into the fatal delusion that his spiritual life may be left to take care of itself, or that God will take care of it, and that there is nothing for him to do. Now the whole teaching of the Bible, as I understand it, is that God takes care of a man's spiritual life as of his mental and physical, by a man's reasonable care of himself;

James i. 19-21. Self-Deception.

o 33

The General Epistle of James

James i. 19-21.

and that that life will perish as truly as the life of a little child born into your home, unless there is this lawful and reasonable care.

Christian Receptivity.

So James begins ver. 19 with the same tender and loving entreaty as ver. 16. He has spoken of the word of truth which God has used as the agent in the regeneration of the Christian Jews. They have heard the word and received it, and the fruit has been spiritual life. Now he seems to say that this same agent is to be employed in sustaining and developing the life. So, 'let every man be *swift to hear*'; or, to use an equivalent term, Let every man be an eager learner, a greedy listener to the truth as it is in Jesus.

The Danger of Contentiousness.

It is apparent that there were some people among the Christian Jews who thought the Christian life would be furthered by discussion; who were evidently much fonder of speaking than of listening; whose speaking grew to angry debating; and that a good deal of miserable ill-will was through their means being engendered. As a matter of fact there are few atmospheres more injurious to the Christian life in its earlier stages than the atmosphere of heated debate and discussion. Now I do not know whether Christian people to-day need to be urged as those people did to be *slow to speak*. It will be evident to us as we proceed that James has a great horror

34

Not Deceived—As to Ourselves

of the sins of the tongue, and that there must **James i. 19-21.** have been a good deal of unlicensed and unbidden and spiteful talking in the Church in his day.

My own impression of the present day is that **Guilty Speech and Guilty Silence.** there is a great deal more of guilty silence than of guilty speaking on spiritual themes. One wishes that people were not quite so slow to speak. But this is certain, that the advice to be swift to hear—to receive with meekness, without prejudice, into an unobstructed heart the implanted word—is both timely and necessary. I do not know of any counsel so valuable to young Christians as this, 'Be diligent learners,' receive into a cleansed heart the word of Christ, let it dwell in you richly. Remember, Christian life consists mainly in receiving, and the man who ceases to receive has nothing to give, and soon has no life. 'As new born babes desire the pure milk of the word.' *Shut your ears to some other things. Store your mind with the word of God.*

See what James declares concerning the Word. **A Gracious Promise.** 'It is able to save your souls.' Probably he refers to the hour of temptation; and as a man may be saved out of an overpowering attack of an enemy, so the Word saves. And he is referring also to the hour of spiritual feebleness, as though a physician should save a life which was fading away, by his

35

The General Epistle of James

James i. 19-21. marvellous prescription. We know what one man said about his Bible: 'Thy word have I hid in mine heart, that I might not sin against Thee.' Men talk of the claims that are made for the Bible to-day. I do not know a greater claim than this, *It is able to save your souls*. It is able, received and acted upon. (But you can disable it by your unbelief.) Its ability has been proved, it is able to save your souls.

The Bible like no other Book. Considering the history of the Bible, apart from all theories of inspiration at present; considering what it has done in enlightening, in comforting, in healing, in saving men; considering its work in the upbuilding of character of a noble and splendid order, we have a right to dispute the claim that it shall be treated as any other book. Find the book that has done anything like what it has done, and you may make the same claim for it. Apart from what it has done for the individual you would find, if you came to search out the secret source of things, that it was the Bible that accounted for the expansion of England in the days of Elizabeth; that it was the Bible that broke the tyranny of the Stuarts and saved England in the time of Oliver Cromwell; that it was the Bible that abolished slavery in Jamaica; that it is the Bible that has ennobled our literature and enriched art and music. On these

Not Deceived—As to Ourselves

grounds alone it is absurd to talk about treating **James i. 19-21.** it as you would any other book.

It is impossible to regard the grey and war-worn veteran, the hero of a hundred fights, in the same way that you regard the newest recruit. No one who is not altogether devoid of the quality of reverence can think of what the Bible has been to innumerable people, and what it has done for countless hosts, without a feeling of reverence for such an instrument springing up in his heart. And it is not an obsolete instrument. *It is able to save your souls.*

VI

NOT DECEIVED—AS TO THE BIBLE

James i. 22-25

But be ye doers of the word, and not hearers only, deluding your own selves. For if any one is a hearer of the word, and not a doer, he is like unto a man beholding his natural face in a mirror: for he beholdeth himself, and goeth away, and straightway forgetteth what manner of man he was. But he that looketh into the perfect law, the *law* of liberty, and so continueth, being not a hearer that forgetteth, but a doer that worketh, this man shall be blessed in his doing.

James i. 22-25. The Bible a Directory. We may be deceived about the Bible, according to the teaching of James ; and herein his teaching is an echo of Christ's. We may think that reverence for the Bible is enough, and especially a reverent reading of the Bible. There may be a great admiration for the Bible, a glow of virtuous feeling at the thought that we know our Bible, and all the time a complete misunderstanding of the real purpose of the Bible.

If the Bible is anything at all, it is a great revelation of human duty, a *great Directory* to which men should turn for guidance, guidance

Not Deceived—As to the Bible

which is to be acted upon, and if it be not, the James i. 22-25.
reader is condemned. The Bible is light coming
from the Father of lights. And it is not in reading the Bible and agreeing with it and loving it,
but in doing it, living in the light, that the value
of the Scripture consists. It is able to save our
souls only as we accept it, and make a determined
effort to live up to its teaching.

James advises people to lay aside *all filthiness* The Bible and Controversy.
and overflowing of wickedness. One of my
Commentaries says that we may freely translate
this, 'disgusting and excessive malignity.' Apparently there were people who so far misjudged
the Bible as to regard it as a fine field for
controversy; they were finding their weapons for
fighting each other in the Bible. There are no
missiles that men have pelted each other with
more frequently and more maliciously than
texts.

You can soon get very angry about the Bible;
and, if you do not watch your heart, very abusive
to the person who differs from you. The word
'filthy' is unfortunately not too strong to apply
to some controversial language and literature on
Biblical questions. A little while ago I held
in my hand a book printed in London in the
seventeenth century, written by a minister of
the Gospel in a great and bitter controversy on

The General Epistle of James

James i. 22-25.

baptism. And the title was, '*Dirt wiped off*; being a reply to a vituperative and abusive pamphlet' of another minister of the Gospel—evidently these two brethren found mud, which they threw heartily at each other, in the Bible.

The Bible and its Readers.

You see what James says. The Word is a mirror in which a man ought to see himself as he is, and be smitten by the sight; and he draws a picture of two men, one, the superficial reader, who mistakes the purpose of the Word, glances at it, goes away—and forgets. The other bends over it, looks into it, finds a law of life in the Word, lives by it, and receives the blessing. Here are two uses of the Bible: (1) Glancing at it, learning nothing; (2) Gazing, doing, receiving the blessing. Happy the man on whom the Word has its full effect; in whose heart, as in good ground, it finds congenial soil and brings forth fruit unto holiness!

VII

NOT DECEIVED—ABOUT RELIGION

JAMES i. 26, 27

IF any man thinketh himself to be religious, while he bridleth not his tongue but deceiveth his heart, this man's religion is vain. Pure religion and undefiled before our God and Father is this, to visit the fatherless and widows in their affliction, and to keep himself unspotted from the world.

A MAN may be deceived *about religion*. It is worth while remarking on the fact that the Book which has more to do with religion than any other book, says almost nothing about religion by name. There are only two other passages in the Bible that I know of where the word occurs. It might be well also to note that James means here the outward acts of religion, the *ritual* rather than the inward spirit, and he desires to set before us what is the true ritual. For a man who had been brought up amid the most elaborate ritual, and who still clung to Temple observances, the language of these verses is certainly very remarkable.

James i. 26, 27. A Christian Ritual.

The General Epistle of James

James i. 26, 27. Unseemly Contrasts. Look at the beginning of verse twenty-six. 'If any man seems to be'—or 'thinks himself to be religious, and . . . deceiveth his own heart.' What a possibility it opens out before us! And how real the possibility is! What standards of religion men have set up! You may read the Bible every day, and say your prayers every night, and have most correct ideas of what is Christian doctrine, *and have an unbridled tongue* —a tongue that runs on in uncharitable censure of other religious people who do not think as you do, in depreciation and denunciation of those professing Christians whose views and habits differ from your own. It is a sad thing when people read the Bible every day, and make a virtue of it, and have none of the virtue of sympathy in their hearts, and do nothing to relieve the misery of their kind. It is for such people that there will be a rude awakening, when the King shall say : 'Inasmuch as ye did it not to one of the least of these, My brethren, ye did it not unto Me.'

The Full Force of Religion. There are some people who stop short at the last sentence in verse twenty-seven, and conclude that if you are only good to the poor you are *ipso facto* religious. To be truly religious, you must carry out the whole verse. You must remember that Paul says : 'Though I bestow

42

Not Deceived—About Religion

all my goods to feed the poor, and have not James i. charity, it profiteth me nothing.' It may not 26, 27. even be philanthropy, it may be penance, or love of self and love of applause, that prompts what you call charity. And even philanthropy is not the whole of religion.

There is another word to go hand in hand Cautions. with this. 'Keep yourself unspotted from the world.' But what is it that spots a Christian character? The world spirit. The love of pleasure spirit. Watch it; keep quite clear of tainted pleasures, pleasures by the production of which some one *is* tainted. Equally tainting is the money-loving spirit.

And guard against introducing a worldly policy into your homes, teaching your children love of dress, love of amusements, and not setting before them the steep pathway of noble and lofty ideals and a simple and unselfish life. Walk in the light as He is in the light. It is possible by divine grace and the cleansing power of the blood of Jesus.

VIII

RESPECT OF PERSONS

JAMES ii. 1-13

MY brethren, hold not the faith of our Lord Jesus Christ, *the Lord* of glory, with respect of persons. For if there come into your synagogue a man with a gold ring, in fine clothing, and there come in also a poor man in vile clothing; and ye have regard to him that weareth the fine clothing, and say, Sit thou here in a good place ; and ye say to the poor man, Stand thou there, or sit under my footstool ; are ye not divided in your own mind, and become judges with evil thoughts? Hearken, my beloved brethren ; did not God choose them that are poor as to the world *to be* rich in faith, and heirs of the kingdom which He promised to them that love Him? But ye have dishonoured the poor man. Do not the rich oppress you, and themselves drag you before the judgement-seats? Do not they blaspheme the honourable name by the which ye are called? Howbeit if ye fufil the royal law, according to the scripture, Thou shalt love thy neighbour as thyself, ye do well: but if ye have respect of persons, ye commit sin, being convicted by the law as transgressors. For whosoever shall keep the whole law, and yet stumble in one *point*, he is become guilty of all. For He that said, Do not commit adultery, said also, Do not kill. Now if thou dost not commit adultery, but killest, thou art become a transgressor of the law. So speak ye, and so do, as men that are to be judged by a law of liberty. For judgement *is* without mercy to him that hath shewed no mercy : mercy glorieth against judgement.

James ii. 1-13. JAMES is a most *practical* writer. He is more of a moralist than a theologian. It will appear clear to you that he has not only a great dread of

Respect of Persons

sins of the tongue, but that he has a very lively **James ii. 1-13.** sense of the dangers which belong to an exaggerated conception of the value of material wealth. He was a poor man, the son of a village carpenter; and he had never lost his respect for the class to which he belonged. And since he had come into the position which he held as chief pastor in the Church at Jerusalem, and had observed the tendency which obtained, even among Christian Jews, to worship wealth, he had been deeply moved. Certainly, the picture which he draws of the Christian Assembly, and its behaviour respecting the rich and the poor, is from a Christian standpoint most humiliating.

The picture, by the way, is very vividly drawn. **The Church Assembled.** You can see the Christian assembly gathered for worship. It consists neither of the rich nor of the very poor. There are chief seats apparently, as there were in the purely Jewish synagogue. It is very doubtful whether there should have been chief seats at all in the Church called by the name of Him who said, 'All ye are brethren'; and it is a comfort that more and more in modern sanctuaries we are doing away with chief seats. But if there were any, they should have been reserved for the holiest men in the Church.

While this congregation is waiting, two visitors **The Two Visitors.**

The General Epistle of James

James ii. 1-13. arrive. With all an Oriental's love of display one is clothed in resplendent apparel; and with obsequious haste these foolish Christians conduct their opulent visitor, who has condescended to appear before the Lord among His people, to the chief place, with a seat of comfort and a footstool for his feet. To the other man who has shuffled in off the street they are barely civil—they do not even offer him a seat. He can stand in a back corner during the service, or he can crouch on the floor, as he is probably accustomed to do in his own miserable hut.

The Deference to Wealth. It is quite apparent that both these people are only visitors to the synagogue. It is at least possible that the poor man has come with mixed motives, perhaps in the hope of enlisting Christian sympathy. But the rich man's motives may be no better. He may have come to the House of the Lord chiefly to display his rich clothing and jewellery. If one came in the hope of receiving alms, the other may have come in the hope of receiving the obsequious flattery and deference of his poorer neighbours. It may have been that if the Lord had given each his place in the synagogue, knowing their hearts, He would have put both in the remotest corner. But the point of the whole narrative is that without reference to character one man is chosen to the chief place,

46

Respect of Persons

the other banished to the obscurest and most contemptible, purely on the ground of social status. There is no need to be rude to the rich man; it is often not his fault that he is rich : it comes from his ancestors, or from his own wonderful endowments, and to be rude and discourteous to him would be foolish and wrong; but to be pointedly discourteous to the poorest, in the sight of Him to whom we are all equal in need, would be a sin.

It is scarcely possible that such a thing as this could happen to-day in any Christian church. But the warning in the opening words of this chapter is needed. By it James seems to say that the two things are incompatible. You may question whether you really hold 'the faith of the Lord Jesus' if you have 'respect of persons.' And he rounds off the paragraph by declaring that we commit *sin*, and break God's law, if we respect persons. It is not, in his inspired judgment, merely a breach of good manners to be discourteous to the poor. It is SIN, as all pride is sin. There may have been some good motive in the way in which the Christians treated the rich man. They may have desired to show him how welcome he was in the Christian assembly. They may have desired to do him good. But it was both mistaken and wrong. As to the rich man,

James ii. 1-13.

Discrimination against the Poor— a Sin.

The General Epistle of James

James ii. 1-13.

if he were sensible, it would defeat their own ends; for he would see through it at once and despise it. It is related of the great Duke of Wellington that on one occasion, as he approached to kneel at the communion rail in a simple village church, a working-man, who knew no better, approached and knelt on the same cushion and at the same time. A horrified official sought to prevent it, and was about to lead the man away, when the Duke forbade it, saying: 'No, no, we are all equal here.'

The Hostility of Rich Jews.

Granted the best possible motive in the treatment of the rich, it was a mistake. The place of all others in the world where one should be taught that 'A man's life consisteth not in the abundance of the things which he possesseth' is the Christian sanctuary. It would appear from verse 6 that the chief trouble of the Jewish Christians arose from the malice of the rich. Their most bitter persecutors and enemies were the rich fellow-countrymen who hated the name of Jesus and blasphemed it, pursuing with vindictive spite those who bore it, and dragging them before the judgment-seats. As a class, the rich were against the Christian faith, though there were honourable exceptions. It is very hard for a rich man to accept the levelling teaching of a Jewish carpenter and the teaching of fishermen, and to be told

48

Respect of Persons

that he was of no more consequence in the sight of God than the poorest; and so, as a class, the rich were bitterly opposed to the Christian faith. It is this fact which imparts, as Dr Dale suggests, a touch of irony to verse 8 : 'If ye are fulfilling the royal law '—if you are doing good to those that do evil to you in your extreme kindness to the rich, you are doing well. But if, on the other hand, 'ye have respect of persons,' ye commit sin and are convicted by the law as transgressors. This conduct was a terribly grave and serious thing, dishonourable to the teaching of Christ, and a disgrace to an assembly called by His name.

This paragraph opens very interesting and instructive considerations for us who form part of the Church of Christ to-day. The rich are no longer the persecutors of the Church of Christ, at least in our own land. But there is no reason why, from a Christian standpoint, they should receive special consideration and honour. A rich man whose heart was touched by the grace of God would despise such court. It would be a pain and an offence to him to be shown into the highest place because of his wealth, and to have his children treated differently from the children of his poorer brethren. He would know that his largest gift could be but a poor return for all the love of God.

The General Epistle of James

**James ii.
1-13.
The Offence
against
the Poor.**

But the chief wrong pointed out in this chapter is the dishonour done to the poor man. *That* is the crying sin. May God deliver us from the miserable vice mentioned in verse 6. We are not to have respect of persons; the word in the original means to look at, and judge by the surface, the appearance, the dress, the house— *literally, the mask*; we are simply to look at character, whether the outer man be rich or poor, and to honour goodness and all who love God, in whatsoever social condition they may be. There should be no cliques or parties in the Church of Christ, no favour shown to social or intellectual superiority; most of all, no scorn for the lowly in position or attainments. *Where that exists, it is a most aggravated form of worldliness,* sternly condemned by the Lord of the Church, the Friend of the poor.

James closed the first chapter by declaring that pure religion is keeping ourselves unspotted from the world. Here is a pure form of worldliness: to flatter the rich, to scorn and despise the poor. It is what the world is doing every day— worshipping the successful, strong, wealthy; and despising the man who is poorer. Let a man fall into that snare, and he is a transgressor of the law, convicted as such by his conduct.

The apostle goes on to *imply*, at least, that it is

Respect of Persons

as grave a matter as though a man had committed **James ii.** one of the mortal sins. 'Whoso shall ... offend **I-13.** in one point, he is guilty of all.'

It seems a hard saying, that of verse 10; it **The Witness** really states a deep moral truth. If a man **of one Offence.** wilfully transgress one commandment, he is breaking the law of obedience which should bind every Christian in bonds of love to God. If a child persisted in disobeying his father's injunction in one particular, he would be a disobedient son; and the very fact of his disobedience would affect his father's judgment of all his conduct. What is more, it would be proof positive that the *spirit* of disobedience was alive and vigorous within him. A true explanation of the passage would not lead you to think of one slip in the hour of temptation. James is speaking rather of a spirit and habit *in one direction*—namely, the dishonour done to the poor—than of a single act; though a single act will often show the underlying spirit, even as a stone piercing through the soil will declare the character of the underlying strata. And no man can wilfully persist in disobedience to God in one point, and fail to be guilty. The disobedience in this one particular vitiates all the rest. It shows the heart unsubdued, the will not given up to God.

To take the matter before us. That Christian

The General Epistle of James

James ii.
1-13.

assembly which James pictures for us on that particular morning may have done many good things. There may have been an excellent sermon and good singing, many prayers and much giving. Perhaps the visit of the gold-fingered man added largely to the Church's offering. But the great fact remained; the Christian law of courtesy and mercy had been violated. In the House of the Lord the poor had been insulted, and that vitiated the whole proceedings and betrayed an anti-Christian spirit.

The need of Self-Scouting.

We often congratulate ourselves on our freedom from the faults and vices of others. It does not follow that we are therefore acceptable to God; faults of another kind equally grave may be in us. Here is a man who never gives way to violent and sullen temper, but he is very careless about speaking the truth. Or he has never owed any man anything; but he has never been known to help anybody in distress. Here is one who has been faithful and affectionate to all his relatives within the home; but who has never lifted a finger to help the world outside. And here is another who has done much outside, and who had better not have done it, because he has been guilty of the grossest neglect and unfaithfulness to those nearest to him. You cannot keep a creditor and debtor account with God. Cling

Respect of Persons

wilfully to any sin, and your whole work is an intolerable offence in His sight, tainted from top to bottom. *James ii. 1-13.*

Two things stand out in solemn clearness at the close of this paragraph. The first is that we are to be judged, and judged in accordance with the law which we have received. It is a law: it comes from the only true *Law-giver*, and when James calls it a 'law of liberty' he probably means that God does not force us by any outward compulsion to obey. The obedience which we bring to Him is to be brought by the free consent of our own heart. He further means that with the law for conduct which God gives us—giving us His love at the same time—He gives us power to obey. And it is by this law, this revelation of love and power, that we shall be judged, and in the light of that judgment our lives are to be ordered. *The Judgment and the Law.*

The second thing that stands out with startling solemnity is that, in the day when men are judged, he that has had no mercy on his fellow-men will receive no mercy from God. It seems a saying hard in its terribleness, but I beg you to observe that it is but an echo of the teaching of Christ (Matt. vi. 14). On that the great teaching of Paul is founded: 'We must all appear before the judgment seat of Christ, that each one may receive the deeds done in his body.' And *The Judgment of the Merciless.*

53

The General Epistle of James

James ii.
1-13.

for the man who has shown no mercy, no compassion, and who, therefore, has lived in absolute antagonism to the divine law, there will be a terrible awakening in the life to come.

54

IX

FAITH AND WORKS

JAMES ii. 14-26

WHAT doth it profit, my brethren, if a man say he hath faith, but have not works? can that faith save him? If a brother or sister be naked, and in lack of daily food, and one of you say unto them, Go in peace, be ye warmed and filled ; and yet ye give them not the things needful to the body ; what doth it profit? Even so faith, if it have not works, is dead in itself. Yea, a man will say, Thou hast faith, and I have works : shew me thy faith apart from *thy* works, and I by my works will shew thee *my* faith. Thou believest that God is one ; thou doest well : the devils also believe, and shudder. But wilt thou know, O vain man, that faith apart from works is barren? Was not Abraham our father justified by works, in that he offered up Isaac his son upon the altar? Thou seest that faith wrought with his works, and by works was faith made perfect; and the scripture was fulfilled which saith, And Abraham believed God, and it was reckoned unto him for righteousness ; and he was called the friend of God. Ye see that by works a man is justified, and not only by faith. And in like manner was not also Rahab the harlot justified by works, in that she received the messengers, and sent them out another way? For as the body apart from the spirit is dead, even so faith apart from works is dead.

HERE we have a famous passage in the epistle, the part that led Luther to pronounce it an epistle of straw. It seems at one point to flatly

James ii. 14-26.

The Teaching of James and of Paul.

The General Epistle of James

James ii. 14-26. contradict the teaching of Paul in Romans iv. But it is at least possible that Luther was mistaken, and that Paul is not contradicting James, but is contradicting those who misunderstood James and distorted his teaching. What one man declares is, that works without faith is dead. The other declares that faith without works is dead. It is more than possible that Paul meant works of a ceremonial order, and James works of a practical order. It is also more than probable that, when Paul speaks of the faith which justifies, he means the lowly personal trust in the Lord Jesus which, when it is genuine, produces good works ; and that James, when he speaks of faith, means an intellectual quality—the holding of an opinion or creed. A faith which, according to verse 19, may be one held by devils, could never be the faith in which Paul lived.

Faith and Works in Harmony. No one can draw the inference from this chapter that James does not teach the necessity of faith. He chooses two conspicuous examples of faith. One, Abraham, who gave up his son in sacrifice, the other, Rahab, who imperilled her life, because they believed. What he declares is, that where faith is genuine, works are sure to follow ; and in verse 18, perhaps the crucial verse of the whole passage, he declares that the only proof of the possession of faith is works, and

Faith and Works

that it is by works, and works only, or by conduct, James ii. and by conduct only, that faith can be exhibited 14-26. —which is only an echo of the teaching of Christ —'Why call ye Me, Lord, Lord, and do not what I say?'

There is a spurious faith; not the lowly trust Spurious in Jesus as Saviour which always results in glad Faith. obedience, but a thing of opinions, creeds, views, and observances, which was precisely what the Pharisees had in the time of Christ. It is like a body without a spirit. It is lacking the warm, vitalising breath of love and child-like trust; where *that* is, there will be the fruits of glad obedience.

By its fruits the tree is known. By your The Tree conduct your spirit is shown, and by your conduct, and its Fruits. not your religious observances, God judges you— conduct, not in the church only, but in your home; not in your home only, but in your social relations with men and women; not in your relations with men and women only, but in your business. Your religious faith is absolutely worthless if it is not daily making you a better man, a better woman, more pure in speech and act, and more merciful. A man may profess to have Christian faith, and be harbouring deeds in his life of which a decent heathen would be ashamed. No one can read the solemn words of

The General Epistle of James

**James ii.
14-26.**

our Lord in Matthew xxv. without seeing that it
is not by opinions but by conduct that men will
be judged. Men who have failed in this are sent
away to the eternal darkness and sorrow.

The whole passage teaches what grave mistakes
may be made by Christian people. How people,
gathered in the name of Christ and bearing His
name, may depart from and violate His Spirit,
and manifest conduct which is a contradiction
and a travesty of the faith which they profess.

Evils as grave as those which apparently
obtained in early Jewish Christian communities
may prevail in Christian communities in England.
The thought should drive us to a closer, a more
reverent and lowly study of the teaching and
spirit of our Lord; and to more earnest and
constant prayer, that He may dwell in the midst
of His Church, and may speak, not only in the
word that is preached, but in the spirit and
conduct of the whole of His professed followers;
that neither discourtesy nor flattery, nor a mere
worship of orthodox opinions, may prevail, or a
body without a spirit, but warm brotherly love of
Him who loved both rich and poor, and desired
to bring them both into the joy of His salvation.

X

ON SPEECH

JAMES iii. 1, 2

BE not many teachers, my brethren, knowing that we shall receive heavier judgement. For in many things we all stumble. If any stumbleth not in word, the same is a perfect man, able to bridle the whole body also.

NOTHING has been said, up to the present, about the style of James. The reading of this chapter forces upon our attention the facts of its *vivid and picturesque character.* He thinks in figures and illumines his theme with metaphors; and some of his figures seem to exaggerate the facts or lessons which he is seeking to bring home to the hearts and consciences of his readers. One has almost wondered whether this austere and just man—in the battles which he must have fought with himself—had been conscious of the tendency to which he refers here, of a violent perversion of the great and noble faculty of speech. Certain it is that he uses extremely strong language, and writes under the stress of deep emotion. You

James iii. 1, 2.

A Writer deeply moved.

59

The General Epistle of James

James iii. 1, 2. see as you read this chapter pictures of a horse curbed by its rider, of a ship in a storm answering to the little rudder at the touch of the steersman, of a forest set ablaze by the careless dropping of a spark or two of fire, and much more.

And all these figures and the strong language which accompanies them are designed to set before us the immense importance of the faculty of speech, by lip or by pen. The importance which he attaches to it may be observed by the fact that it is not dwelt on in this chapter alone; in chap. i. 19 and chap. iv. 11 also, he deals with the same subject, and demands our careful study.

We should be unfair to the significance of this chapter if we failed to notice its obvious local application. It is quite apparent from the letter, that there was a great deal of ill-considered, ill-natured, self-assertive and violent speech among Jewish Christians; a good deal of angry debating and bitter strife. We may deal with that for a moment first of all.

The Early Christian Assemblies. We saw in our last study a picture of the Christian assembly. It was very different from our own Christian assemblies. Here we quietly listen while one man unfolds to us what he has found in the word of God. We have not gone quite to the other extreme from the condition which obtained in the Christian synagogue. In

60

On Speech

the early Christian assemblies, according to St Paul's picture, there was often no authorised teacher or leader, and there was consequent confusion ; numbers of men and women clamouring to speak at the same time, and perhaps claiming to be moved by the Holy Ghost. So that Paul declares that two, or at most three, shall speak in order (1 Cor. xiv. 26-33).

James iii. 1, 2.

It is with the Christian assembly as he knew it that James deals, and it is evident that there was a great and a strong tendency in this assembly towards speaking and debating. Heated discussions were the order of the day. Every man had his opinions, which he was eager to thrust on the assembly, not for its profit so much as for his own notoriety, and his word in the first chapter, 'Let every man be swift to hear—slow to speak,' must be considered in the light of this state of things.

Profitless Clamour.

He advises them to meditate well over what they have heard, and not to speak until they have quite grasped its full meaning. I suppose the class of people James had in mind were those mentioned by Paul—vain talkers, 'desiring to be teachers of the law, though they understand neither what they say nor whereof they confidently affirm.'

XI

ON THE TEACHER

JAMES iii. 1, 2

BE not many teachers, my brethren, knowing that we shall receive heavier judgement. For in many things we all stumble. If any stumbleth not in word, the same is a perfect man, able to bridle the whole body also.

James iii. 1, 2. IT must be understood that James believes in the teaching office. Men are to be 'swift to hear,' and they can be thus only as there is some one to speak.

The Responsibility of the Teacher. What he declares in this first verse is the solemn responsibility of the Christian teacher; and what he seems to say is, that it is a position that men need not clamour for, nor take on themselves lightly. There is terrible judgment for the man who is idle and unfaithful in the office of the Christian teacher, who will not take the trouble of patiently and laboriously investigating the meaning of the word which he expounds, who aims at popularity or smartness, seeking his own glory or some superficial success. And there is terrible judgment for the man

On the Teacher

who mixes personal animosity, bitterness, malice, James iii. impatience and resentment with his teaching; 1, 2. who is more anxious to score a personal victory than to understand and make clear the will of God.

There is a sense in which every Christian teacher, in pulpit, class or home should be slow to speak. The themes with which he deals are so immense and sublime, that glib, ill-considered speech, shallow assumptions, and dogmatic pronouncements are to be dreaded. Every lesson, every message on the nature of God and of sin, its redemption and punishment, needs to be well pondered and steeped in prayer.

Probably there is not a rush to-day, as there Teachers was apparently in the early Church, for the needed. position of a teacher of spiritual things. But teachers are always needed. All Christian mothers and fathers should feel it their duty and privilege to instruct their children in spiritual things; it is perfectly appalling that children should grow up without definite religious instruction. We always need to plead for people who will enter the solemn and blessed calling of the Christian teacher; but all of us who are in it need to realise the necessity of living a prayerful, pure and earnest life, to keep ourselves beneath the illuminating influence of the Holy Ghost.

The General Epistle of James

James iii. 1, 2. The Dangers of Silence. Perhaps on spiritual matters it might be urged to-day that our danger lies in the direction of silence rather than that of speech. It is difficult to persuade even Christian people to enter upon a discussion on purely spiritual themes, and parents speak far too little on these themes to their children. We need to realise that we may sin by silence as well as by speech. 'No man can look back on his past life, and fail to see that not once nor twice his supreme duty was a word, and through cowardice or unreadiness his guilt was that he spoke not.'[1]

The Shame of Guilty Silence. Many of us have felt the shame of being straitened in prayer, of being too timid to say 'No' to the tempter, and to speak out the brave reasons of which the heart was full. We have many of us through shame allowed the conversation to take an unworthy turn; failed to utter the word of warning which might have saved a soul from going in the wrong direction; and found ourselves only able to stammer when the circumstances demanded a clear and loud testimony. Carlyle, himself the prophet of silence, the advocate of deeds as against words, says: 'If the word is not there, you have no man there either, but a phantasm instead.' We want people who will speak, but who will speak

[1] G. H. Smith, *Comm. on Isai.*, vol. i.

On the Teacher

because they have thought, and pondered and prayed over and known the truth which they declare, and whose word will bear the judgment of the righteous God. [James iii. 1, 2.]

You may for a moment compare verse 2 with ch. ii. 10, for the different meanings of the word 'stumble.' This is an occasional fall; that, a persistent course of disobedience to one point of the law; and the latter part of this verse really declares that when a man has learnt to rule his tongue absolutely, he is a master in the art of self-government. Government of the tongue is the distinct and decisive mark of self-government.

XII

THE CONTROL OF THE TONGUE

JAMES iii. 3-8

Now if we put the horses' bridles into their mouths, that they may obey us, we turn about their whole body also. Behold, the ships also, though they are so great, and are driven by rough winds, are yet turned about by a very small rudder, whither the impulse of the steersman willeth. So the tongue also is a little member, and boasteth great things. Behold, how much wood is kindled by how small a fire! And the tongue is a fire: the world of iniquity among our members is the tongue, which defileth the whole body, and setteth on fire the wheel of nature, and is set on fire by hell. For every kind of beasts and birds, of creeping things and things in the sea, is tamed, and hath been tamed by mankind: but the tongue can no man tame; *it is* a restless evil, *it is* full of deadly poison.

James iii. 3-8. NOWHERE that I know of is the difficulty of controlling the temper more vividly set forth. Man is skilled in taming all kinds of creatures, beasts and birds and creeping things, and things in the sea; but no man can tame the tongue. By which James does not mean, I take it, that the world has never seen a man in whom the faculty of speech is under perfect control—he could

The Control of the Tongue

scarcely say that, with the example of John before him; but rather where you have a person of unrestrained and violent speech there is no power on earth that can subdue and control it. Many of us will probably sympathise with the teaching, and feel an echo of it in our own consciences.

James iii. 3-8.

Our tongue has a way of running on uncontrolled by thought, it tells confidences which ought never to be divulged. It escapes our control and runs all unchecked over the affairs of our neighbours, detracting, depreciating, suspecting, suggesting, or scorning and holding up to ridicule. It is not governed by reverence or dignity; and it often runs on into actually low, vulgar and coarse speech, speech that lacks refinement; even into absolute folly. And all the time we are unconscious that we are really debasing a great and noble instrument and perverting a great faculty, besides lowering the tone of the society in which we move, and sending a stream over the lives of others—children and younger people—that will leave a most unwholesome sediment behind it. And if there is difficulty in governing a loose tongue, in importing thoughtfulness and reverence and goodwill and refinement into speech, how much more difficult is it to refrain from *angry, resentful* speech!

The Tongue Uncontrolled.

67

The General Epistle of James

James iii. 3-8. The Tongue Controlled. I do not think James desiderates here what you would call a tame tongue. Certainly his own style is the very reverse of that; it leaps and bounds with the utmost vigour. What he brings before us here rather is a fiery steed under perfect control, answering to the bit of its rider—full of movement, but under law—or a ship, driven by most fierce winds, but answering to the rudder and obeying the will of the steersman. Let a man be thus, and he may still have fiery and vehement speech.

But the difficulty is to obtain this control. There are some lines which come to the writer as a memory of childhood, and with more point than poetry express the difficulty :—

> 'Flat contradiction can you bear
> When you are right, and know you are,
> Nor flatly contradict again?
> But wait and modestly explain,
> And show your reasons one by one,
> Nor think of triumph when you've done.'

'Not Answering again.' And Paul puts the matter to servants who may be ill-treated, in his letter to Titus. 'Not answering again.' How many of us are equal to that, when a stinging or cutting remark is made, when an unjust statement is made, when we are undeservedly blamed, credited with wrong that we have never done? Or, on the contrary, how

68

The Control of the Tongue

many of us are determined to have the last word; and how often under such circumstances our tongue escapes our control and becomes an untamed creature, full of deadly poison, setting on fire the whole of our nature, and being itself set on fire of hell! *James iii. 3-8.*

It may seem to some of us that James speaks too strongly here, that his own tongue is not under control. But a moment's reflection will convince us, and a remembrance of some of the most humiliating experiences of our lives will assure us, of the fact that, on those rare occasions when we have succeeded in controlling the tongue by desperate effort and earnest prayer—when we have been silent under provocation, or have answered with quiet dignity as a Christian should —the effect of the victory has been felt throughout our whole life. Here is a word for us all. 'I said I will take heed to my ways, that I sin not with my tongue: I will keep my mouth with a bridle.' 'Keep Thou the door of my lips.' *A Victory worth Achieving.*

By the side of the difficulty of controlling must be placed the possible evils that may be wrought by uncontrolled speech. It is scarcely necessary to dwell at length on these. There is no passage in literature which more vehemently sets forth these evils than verse 6. Remember, it is only one side that James deals with, there is a corres- *Evil that may be Wrought.*

The General Epistle of James

James iii. 3-8. pondingly noble side to the faculty of speech. He must have been wrought upon by the amount of evil-speaking going on in the Hebrew Church, to write so strongly. But the possibilities of which he speaks are very real.

Pollution. There is, first of all, the effect of speech on the man who makes it. It defileth the whole man. Some other words are recalled. 'Not that which goeth into the man defileth the man; but that which cometh out.' We have a theory that if a thing be in the heart, it may as well be spoken. It is fatally wrong. You sully your lips, and degrade your whole nature, when you suffer yourself to speak the tainted and tainting word. Just as the utterance of a noble conviction strengthens and lifts up the whole being, so the utterance of a foul thing debases it, and plunges the whole nature into the mire. The whole course of your nature can be set on fire with an unwholesome and devouring lust by the spoken word.

Wronging Others. Still more important is the effect it may have on others. A whispered word may take away a reputation. Ill-considered and loose speech on the part of a Christian teacher may lead souls to destruction. Start a slander on its way, and before you can overtake it, it may smirch the character of half a dozen men. Give your ill-

The Control of the Tongue

considered or distorted opinion that a certain James iii. course is right—which you would see to be wrong 3-8. if you prayed about it, and you may lead a multitude into ways of evil. Let a foul word escape your lips, and it may be like a whiff of poisonous gas from a sewer, which poisons the blood of every passer-by. Just a word, an ill-considered, malicious, slanderous, lustful, ill-natured word, dropped without thought or intention, as one would drop a lighted match, and the result is the destruction of a noble and stately forest. The evil is started, and no man can overtake it.

XIII

POSSIBILITIES OF EVIL
AND BLESSING

James iii. 9-12

THEREWITH bless we the Lord and Father; and therewith
curse we men, which are made after the likeness of God: out
of the same mouth cometh forth blessing and cursing. My
brethren, these things ought not so to be. Doth the fountain
send forth from the same opening sweet *water* and bitter? can
a fig tree, my brethren, yield olives, or a vine figs? neither
can salt water yield sweet.

**James iii.
9-12.
Possibilities.**
No one can over-estimate the power of speech.
The greatest victories for right and wrong have
been won by it. Every day it is being plied
between man and man, teacher and taught. Oh,
if it could be cleansed of all exaggeration, of all
lying in commerce! If every business circular
and advertisement said what it meant, and meant
what it said! If our daily press were cleansed
of all misrepresentation. If it described things
exactly as they are! If people who rush into
controversy and wish to make their voices heard,
would take the trouble to acquaint themselves

72

Possibilities of Evil and Blessing

with facts and then to represent them accurately ! **James iii. 9-12.**
If in social life speech could be cured of unreality
and unkindness ! If our speech were less trifling,
and dealt with greater themes, what a change
would come over the whole of society ! How is
it all to be done ? Well, we must each begin with
ourselves.

Judgment must begin at the house of God.
That is a terrible picture that James draws in
verse 9.

It has been true to life at many periods of
Christian history. The lips that affected to
bless God in prayer have been turned away to
curse men. No louder or deeper curses have
been uttered probably than have come from the
lips of ecclesiastics. I suppose James had heard
of Church members cursing those who differed
from them. And he suggests in verses 11 and **The Witness of the Tongue.**
12, that the deep-lying cause of unregenerate
speech is an unregenerate nature. We recall the
words of ch. i. 26 : 'If any man seemeth to be
religious, and bridleth not his tongue . . . this
man's religion is in vain.' So he suggests that
Christian faith and uncontrolled speech are
incompatible. If a tree bring forth olives, it is
not a fig tree. And no fountain will bring forth
sweet and bitter, salt water and fresh. The
deep-lying suggestion is that the heart is wrong

The General Epistle of James

James iii. 9-12. where the speech is wrong; and that if the fires of hell have kindled a man's tongue, they are in his nature; for it is ever true that out of the abundance of the heart the mouth speaketh. Foul speech never came from a pure heart, nor did slanderous and bitter speech ever emanate from a soul filled with Divine Love; though the heart that is a cage of unclean birds and filled with hatred, can cover it with fair and apparently loving speech. We shall not curse men, nor send forth bitter torrents of cruel words, if our hearts are in God's keeping, and we live in the full consciousness of His presence.

The Tongue's Opportunities. How great are the possibilities of a tongue which is under Divine control, cleansed and anointed! What sorrows it can comfort, what wounds it can heal, what strife it can still! How it can woo and persuade men into the ways of goodness, and change the current of evil-thinking! How it can hearten the depressed, and encourage the downcast and reprove the evil-doer! How it can make men ashamed of evil, and kindle purest and holiest desire! What music there is in the pure prattle of a child, and the quiet tones of a gentle-hearted wife and mother! For, corresponding with the possibilities of evil in speech, are the possibilities of good. It is such an effective weapon that the devil seeks to capture it and

Possibilities of Evil and Blessing

use it for doing his deadly work. But it is also James iii. God's mightiest instrument for the pulling down 9-12. of the strongholds of sin, and the upbuilding of His kingdom.

It is not without perpetual significance that when the Holy Ghost descended upon the disciples, the sign was that of tongues of fire— the fire of divine love. And all that is best in the use of the tongue may be ours. Not noble eloquence, perhaps, but pure, true, loving speech from a pure, true, loving heart, controlled by the Spirit of God.

XIV

WISDOM, TRUE AND FALSE

James iii. 13-16

Who is wise and understanding among you? let him shew by his good life his works in meekness of wisdom. But if ye have bitter jealousy and faction in your heart, glory not and lie not against the truth. This wisdom is not *a wisdom* that cometh down from above, but is earthly, sensual, devilish. For where jealousy and faction are, there is confusion and every vile deed.

James iii. 13-16. We have before us a passage which it is not easy to expound. We need to remember that it was written to Christians, and its first force, and, if I may say so, its first fire, must fall upon and search the Christian heart. May you and I, dear reader, be able to take, not an intellectual interest, but a heart interest in it, and may the Spirit of God both illumine and make willing our hearts while we study this word!

The passage begins with a question : ' Who is wise and understanding among you?' And if we may judge from the tone of the earlier part of the letter, and think of the people clamouring

76

Wisdom, True and False

to make themselves heard, and seeking to win **James iii. 13-16.** verbal victories over others, we must imagine that the answer, 'We are,' would come from the lips of many.

So he proceeds to sketch in outline false and **Wisdom— False and True.** true wisdom, and to show in what they severally consist. 'If you are really wise,' he says, 'you will show the fact by a "good conversation"'— which could be more accurately translated 'a beautiful life'—and the chief adornment of a truly wise life is meekness or modesty. Apparently these people had another ideal of wisdom —wisdom to them meant being clever enough to get their own way, sharp enough to confound an opponent in debate, and to win a verbal victory over him.

It is a very sad picture which he draws in verse 14. He has been speaking in the previous paragraph of an untamed tongue—a tongue which is a restless evil, and full of deadly poison, 'set on fire of hell,' and he seems to say in this paragraph: 'Such a tongue has behind it a heart that is full of poison.' The fountain is sending forth bitter water (verse 11). It is because it is itself full of bitterness, the bitterness of jealousy. Envenomed speech comes out of an envenomed heart.

And this is what James seems to say, if I may **The Motive and Spirit of Contention.** paraphrase him for a moment. 'If you have

The General Epistle of James

James iii. 13-16. bitter jealousy in your heart, under the pressure of that fierce fire you may score a victory over an opponent, and humble him. You may even be fighting on the right side as against one who is mistaken and wrong. But there is nothing to boast about, nor to glory over. It is a victory not for truth, but for malice. And you cannot pretend to holiness. You must not lay claim to virtue; if you do, you "lie against the truth." Your battle was fought with a bad weapon. You may think that you are a brave warrior against error, but if your warfare has been dictated by personal envy, bitter jealousy or personal ambition, you have injured your cause by your spirit.'

Wrong Motives. Should it not come home to our hearts, brethren, in a time of controversy, that a man may possibly fight in a most righteous cause, not because he loves justice supremely, and wants to get right done, not even because he understands the cause in which he fights, but because he loves a fight, and is naturally contentious and bitter-spirited, and envious of others; or because he has an unquenchable thirst for notoriety and pre-eminence and personal triumph? We can smirch the purest cause by a foul motive. What this striking passage seems to me to teach is, that no matter what the cause may be, where there is bitter jealousy and strife and envy in the heart,

Wisdom, True and False

the acts proceeding from the heart are unworthy. **James iii. 13-16.** Your cause may be good, you may win the victory over your opponent, but neither you nor your action are good.

Bitter jealousy, how easy it is to get it! The **Jealousy.** poor against the rich, the failing man against the successful and prosperous, the competitor against his rival! How we need to watch our hearts! How we need to humble ourselves severely before God!

You have heard of men who could never brook a rival, who pursued with relentless hate those who they imagined had injured them. You have heard of men in places of business who eyed with vigilant jealousy every aspirant to an equal position to their own. You have heard of parties and cliques and bitter divisions in the Christian Church itself ever since the days of the Church in Corinth.

You have heard of men, nay, have we not felt them to be very near to our own hearts, who spoke depreciatory words at every convenient opportunity concerning their neighbours in business—and God forgive us for it—even in Christian service? Have we never felt resentment, dislike or the inclination to speak uncharitably and contemptuously of people, because they differed from us in their conception of the Christian life ; and

79

The General Epistle of James

James iii.
13-16.

if we searched our motives to their secret depths, would we not be bound to confess that we have sometimes, Christians though we are, disliked people and spoken slightingly and ill of them because they were better than we, more prayerful, more spiritually-minded, more truly set on Divine things? I must confess that I read verse 15 with a trembling heart, with its characterisation of the kind of spirit which I have tried to describe. There is no mincing of words with this man. Paul says the spirit is carnal—James says it is worldly, animal, devilish. *There* is a form of worldliness which I have to watch against. It is inevitable that I must fight, but I am to fight as a Christian, without any trace of personal malignity or bitter strife.

XV

DIVINE WISDOM

JAMES iii. 17

BUT the wisdom that is from above is first pure, then
peaceable, gentle, easy to be intreated, full of mercy and
good fruits, without variance, without hypocrisy.

IT is with the greatest possible relief that I turn **James iii.**
to the exquisite picture which James draws of **17.**
true and divine wisdom, the quality of heart **Divine Wisdom:**
which he has urged us to pray for in the first **Its Characteristics.**
chapter. Will you mark the outline of this
exquisite portrait? (1) It is *pure* first and most **Purity.**
of all; clean, that is, with no alloy of self-will;
pure and sweet and true in motive. It wants
only the good, whether it win or lose, a quality
closely allied to holiness. 'Free from guilt, without spot or blemish,' so the word is defined in my
Greek lexicon. And (2) it is *peaceable.* It must **Peaceableness.**
fight; but it fights for the sake of peace, and
knows that there can never be true peace until
there is righteousness. But it is the very reverse
of quarrelsome and contentious; and all the time

F 81

The General Epistle of James

James iii. 17. it is fighting it hungers for peace, and will heal all divisions by wise and generous words.

Gentleness. (3) *Gentle* comes from a word difficult to translate into English. It means equity, reasonableness, considerateness towards others, the power to see their side of things, as well as one's own. It is *tractable* also, easy to be intreated, not stubborn; not, as Dr Dale suggests, refusing to do a thing simply because one has been asked to do it; a military word, meaning one who can keep rank with his comrades and march along in the same path.

Mercy, Fruitfulness, Sincerity. It is moreover (4) '*full of mercy and good fruits*'; it is *single-minded* and *absolutely sincere*. It is an exquisite delineation of character, so fascinatingly attractive that it wins us by its charms, while it seems so high above us in its pure loveliness as to be impossible of attainment. There is not a sincere soul among us that does not long to be clothed with this spirit.

The Source of Divine Wisdom. The first line of verse 17 indicates clearly its source. It is from *above*; it is acquired in communion with the Highest, in fellowship with God —a thing we are sadly neglecting. We are trying to be and do good; we are distressed more or less for our faults. We have lost to a large extent, it is to be feared, the holy art of fellowship with God. If the question were passed round

82

Divine Wisdom

any considerable number of Christian people, 'Is communion with God a fact of your life?' it is impossible to say how many could answer it in the affirmative. And yet it is just this question which we should force ourselves to face. Without this communion there is no true Christian living, and strangers to it can never acquire noble Christian character. It is the source of true wisdom.

James iii. 17.

XVI

THE THIRST FOR PLEASURE

JAMES iii. 18; iv. 1-4

AND the fruit of righteousness is sown in peace for them that make peace. Whence *come* wars and whence *come* fightings among you? *come they* not hence, *even* of your pleasures that war in your members? Ye lust, and have not: ye kill, and covet, and cannot obtain: ye fight and war; ye have not, because ye ask not. Ye ask, and receive not, because ye ask amiss, that ye may spend *it* in your pleasures. Ye adulteresses, know ye not that the friendship of the world is enmity with God?

James iii. 18; iv. 1-4. OBSERVE the abrupt contrast between ch. iii. 18 and ch. iv. 1.

Righteousness: Its Origins. In the first James speaks of peace, deep-lying peace, an angel of God that has departed from some of us; he says that the 'fruit of righteousness is sown in peace,' by which statement we may infer that it is never sown in war. There are very few wars of nations in the history of the world in which the fruit of righteousness was sown. The quarrelsome temper is scarcely ever the temper that makes for or produces

84

The Thirst for Pleasure

righteousness. It is the calm, equable, self-controlled, God-controlled soul that is calculated to produce righteousness. **James iii. 18; iv. 1-4.**

Then abruptly from the picture of peace James turns to that of war, the wretched janglings and discords that evidently prevail among them, and he asks whence they come? What is their origin? And this is his answer: They come of your pleasures—probably your thirsts for pleasure which are encamped in your members. These thirsts should be kept under rigid control; but they have broken bounds; they are *encamped* in your members; the lower side of you has vanquished the higher. **Discord; Its Origins.**

The question might be asked: 'What do the love of pleasure, the love of amusement, the love of money, the love of display war against?' And mark you that love may be hotly cherished in the heart where there are no means of satisfying it. It may burn as a suppressed and unholy fire there, and may become fiercely envious and jealous of those who have the power to indulge it. Well, these pleasures will *war against our delight in spiritual things*. They may so master us that all spiritual things will stand for us in the realm of duty, irksome and disagreeable duty, things in which there isno pleasure, and which we must turn away from in order to get pleasure. **The Thirst for Pleasure. Harmful to Spirituality.**

85

The General Epistle of James

James iii. 18; iv. 1-4. My strong impression is that one of our modern Christian failures is the failure to see *the sweet and abundant joy that there is in spiritual exercises.* It is possible that if we searched our hearts honestly we should discover that the thirst for pleasure is weakening and destroying our thirst for God.

Harmful to Others. But these pleasures ruling in us *war against those around us.* That is an alarming expression in verse 2 : '*Ye kill.*' Dr Dale thinks we may take it literally, and think of people who are so determined on securing outward good and pleasure that they unscrupulously over-ride, and break the hearts of, those who stand in their pathway. Others think it means the cherishing of hateful thoughts.

The Passion for Self-Indulgence. Anyhow, it is an appalling picture that the writer draws, the picture of people who are not praying, or who, even when they pray, ask only for selfish ends, for outward good, that they may spend it extravagantly upon their pleasures. It is, I say, an appalling picture of people thirsting for worldly good as the supreme good of life, baffled in their pursuit, either disappointed in the pleasure they expected to find in worldly good, or in the good itself, and becoming envious and bitter in their spirits, and even in their prayers, towards those who are more successful than

86

The Thirst for Pleasure

themselves. The apostle sums it all up in James iii. a phrase which I do not know whether the men 18; iv. 1-4. of this generation will accept, namely, *that the friendship of the world is enmity with God.*

XVII

FRIEND OF THE WORLD
OR OF GOD

JAMES iv. 4-6

WHOSOEVER therefore would be a friend of the world maketh himself an enemy of God. Or think ye that the Scripture speaketh in vain ? Doth the spirit which He made to dwell in us long unto envying ? But He giveth more grace.

James iv. 4-6.
A Parlous State.

THIS passage begins with one of the startling sayings in a most startling paragraph; it suggests that a Christian man may be drawn, may glide, almost unconsciously, into a condition of enmity with God. It recalls one of the most moving passages of St Paul. *'Many walk'*—he is speaking of professing Christian people — *' of whom I have told you often, and now tell you even weeping, that they are the enemies of the cross of Christ'*; and his description of them ends with his phrase *'who mind earthly things.'* That is their final aim—earthly gains, earthly pleasures, sensuous delights, while the things of the soul are neglected, and everything that savours of the cross is slighted and despised. It resolves itself

88

Friend of the World or of God

into this, that instead of dwelling in the love of God and the will of God, and finding a delight in that will, we consult our own will, and follow our own inclinations, and live for the pleasure of the passing moment. *James iv. 4-6.*

One is bound to confess that there is a vast difference between the way in which our fathers regarded the world, and the way in which we regard it. Isaac Watts called it a 'vile' world in one of his best-known hymns. A man would almost need to apologise for using such a phrase nowadays. He would be accounted bigoted and pharisaical, if he said : 'We know that we are of God, little children, and the whole world lieth in the wicked one.' It sounds terribly harsh ; but it is Scripture, and James asks whether the Scripture speaks in vain. What is the world? Well, it is that order of things about us, or that spirit in us which is blind and deaf to the value and reality of spiritual things, and careless to the will of God. It is that spirit which is governed by the desires of the flesh or by the fashions and customs around us, and does not consult and submit itself to the will of God, and acknowledge His right to rule us. *The Church and the World.*

We may all glide into that. The world seems such a harmless, attractive, exciting, gay creature, wreathed in smiles and laughter, carrying in her *The Allurement of the World.*

89

The General Epistle of James

James iv. 4-6. hands such a wealth of delights, that hearts are often subtly won from their allegiance to God. If we think very highly of the world, and its amusements are more diverting than spiritual exercises to us, that, says James, *is unfaithfulness.* That is what he means by the term *'adulterers.'*

A Plea for Fidelity to God. The Church is the bride of Christ. Israel was the wooed and won bride of God. James was steeped in all Old Testament teaching, and worldliness to him was unfaithfulness; and unfaithfulness is really the worst kind of enmity. Like one of the Old Testament prophets his voice takes a tenderer tone, and he draws for us a picture which perhaps more surely than strong language is calculated to move the heart and conscience and turn it again towards God. The picture is obscured by ambiguous language, but to my mind Mr Mayor is correct in rendering it: 'The spirit which He made to dwell in us jealously yearns for our entire devotion.' (See R. V. margin.) The passage again recalls the words of Paul (2 Cor. xi. 2): 'For I am jealous over you with a godly jealousy: for I espoused you to one husband, that I might present you as a pure virgin to Christ.' It recalls also words of the old law: 'Thou shalt have no other God before Me, for I, the Lord thy God, am a jealous God.' And the idea is that of the intense longing of Divine Love to possess the

90

Friend of the World or of God

whole soul; to be loved with an undivided **James iv. 4-6.**
heart.

Wives and mothers can understand this, and **The Yearning of God for us.** God has been pleased to reveal Himself to us by means of these relations. You know perfectly well that intense love longs for response: that nothing in the world is so sweet as that response; and that no pain is so tragic and agonising as the pain caused by the alienation of the affection, the fact of the loved one carrying his confidences elsewhere, and committing his trouble to other ears, and accepting other guidance. It is all a feeble picture of the yearning of God over each one of us, and the pain whenever our love is withheld. It is not that God longs for your obedience—mere power might do that. Love hungers for love, and God, because of the great love wherewith He has loved us, hungers for our love. Oh, that we could realise it, and realising it give ourselves whole-heartedly to the service of our Lord!

XVIII

HUMBLE SUBMISSION TO GOD

JAMES iv. 6-10

BUT He giveth more grace. Wherefore *the Scripture* saith, God resisteth the proud, but giveth grace to the humble. Be subject therefore unto God ; but resist the devil, and he will flee from you. Draw nigh to God. and He will draw nigh to you. Cleanse your hands, ye sinners; and purify your hearts, ye double-minded. Be afflicted, and mourn, and weep : let your laughter be turned to mourning, and your joy to heaviness. Humble yourselves in the sight of the Lord, and He shall exalt you.

James iv. 6-10. WE have to remember that this passage follows one of the heaviest indictments made in the Bible.

An Accusation and an Appeal. A charge, which reminds us in its severity, of some of the Old Testament prophecies, has been brought against the Jewish Christians; a charge of unfaithfulness to God, and enmity to man. The law of the King : 'Thou shalt love the Lord thy God with all thy heart, and soul, and mind, and strength, and thy neighbour as thy thyself,' had been flagrantly violated by men bearing the

92

Humble Submission to God

Christian name. It was a most serious charge, and St James seems to lash them unsparingly, almost fiercely, as he drives it home. Then he concludes with the most moving picture of God yearning with unspeakable desire for the *entire* devotion of the fickle heart—not giving it up— but, in spite of unfaithfulness, waiting and giving. Twice in this sixth verse He is represented as the *giving* God, whose grace abounds even where sin abounds.

James iv. 6-10.

But the grace of God is never intended to make men think lightly of sin. Whenever that is done, there has been a most serious misunderstanding of God's grace. There is a way out—let us thank God for it—of unfaithfulness and sin, and the clutches of an evil power that has captured us; but it is not by thinking lightly of unfaithfulness, by glossing it over with excusing words. The way out is indicated in verse 10, which is the keynote of this passage: 'Humble yourselves *in the sight of the Lord.*' They had drifted right away from God—a worldly spirit had captured them, an evil spirit had laid hold of them, greed of gain, love of the world, malice, hatred, and all uncharitableness had fastened themselves upon their hearts. Here is the way out of it all: 'Humble yourselves in the sight of God.'

A Plea for Self-Humbling.

Now, it would probably not be difficult to

93

The General Epistle of James

James iv. 6-10. bring home to the hearts of most of us a consciousness that we have not rendered the loving obedience which it is our duty to render; that the spirit of the world and the spirit of evil has **Reasons for such Humbling.** mastered us; that we, too, have been unfaithful to God, to whom we all belong, and that our allegiance to Him has wavered and broken. At this very moment, perhaps, our thoughts and desires are not set on the ways of obedience to His will. We have broken again and again His law of love; we have not even troubled to consult His will, though we are called Christians; we go for days without even asking whether this act, or that habit, or the other line of conduct, are in accordance with His will for us—we know that it suits our inclination, or that it is customary, and there is no great harm in it, and we have not concerned ourselves with anything besides. The charges of the former part of this chapter, if they were forced home, would find an echo, as far at least as the spirit of them is concerned, in many of our consciences.

The Resistance to Penitence. But it is to be questioned very seriously whether anything could bring us the intense grief and mourning and sorrow which St James urges in verse 9. Is it not true that at times we even discourage depression, mourning and sadness concerning sin; that, instead of welcoming peni-

94

Humble Submission to God

tence, we fight it off in ourselves and in others, until tears and agony on account of unfaithfulness to God are becoming exceedingly rare amongst us? Should any manifest signs of distress, we think they are out of health, and we suggest change of air, a tonic, a stimulant, a visit to the sea, or a course of amusements; and we tell people that there is no need to distress themselves about their failures, because everybody fails, and God is merciful! *James iv. 6-10.*

It is by no means certain that we are either right or wise. May be, the best that could happen to us would be a little wholesome grief about our spiritual condition. Our bane is our self-complacency; our constant habit of excusing and making light of our failings and sins, and disloyalty to Christ. We say we believe in the Divine mercy. So did the inspired writers of the Scriptures. It would be a daring claim that we had a more true or radiant conception of the love of God than they had. James believed in and knew the grace and mercy of God; and because he knew it, and knew how men had sinned against it, he urges the most complete grief and distress. *A Mistaken Policy.*

Please observe that his whole endeavour in this paragraph is to bring men face to face with God. They have not merely to consider their

95

The General Epistle of James

James iv. 6-10.
Can you face God thus?

conduct, and try to make it better. First of all, they have to consider Him. Note how the verses begin: 'Be subject unto God' (7). 'Draw nigh to God' (8). 'Humble yourselves in the sight of the Lord' (10). Am I not right in saying that this is another point in which we modern people fail? Even the man who professes to believe in a large and general way in the mercy of God, who would say: 'I must try to do better henceforth' (as though that disposed of the matter), who would fight against evil and sin, would shrink from coming face to face with God. Yet that is surely James' point. You have to deal with God. You have broken with Him, you have been unfaithful to Him, you have been double-minded, half for God, and half for self. You can do nothing until you have made it right with Him, until your relation to Him is harmonious, until your estrangement to Him healed.

There is silence and a cloud between your soul and Him, and it must be broken. He yearns over you; turn and submit yourself to Him. Get rid of double-mindedness. Him you have forsaken, yet to Him you belong.

XIX

A DANGER AND A REMEDY

JAMES iv. 11, 12

SPEAK not one against another, brethren. He that
speaketh against a brother, or judgeth his brother, speaketh
against the law, and judgeth the law : but if thou judgest
the law, thou art not a doer of the law, but a judge. One
only is the lawgiver and judge, *even* He who is able to save and
to destroy : but who art thou that judgest thy neighbour ?

LET us look again for a moment at verses 6-10, **James iv.**
observe the method of thought; it is important. **11, 12.**
There are some people who try to 'resist the **Some Mistakes**
devil' without having come into subjection to God. **made.**
There are some who try to 'cleanse their hands,'
before they draw nigh to God. There are some
who weep over their faults, and afflict their souls
without having sought to draw nigh to God.
There are some who try to 'lift themselves up,'
to use the phrase of verse 10 ; either to banish a
pensive and repentant mood, or to make themselves a little more presentable before they return
to God. It is a wrong method, and results in
failure. Drawing nigh to God with all your

G   97

The General Epistle of James

**James iv.
II, 12.** faults on you, subjecting the will to Him in humble obedience, is *the very first thing*. Then, when that is done, you may hope to successfully resist the devil. It is the soul that has got rid of double-mindedness, and is given-over to God in complete obedience, that successfully resists temptation. 'In the covert of His wings there is sure defence.' You cannot fight against evil effectively excepting as your soul is in harmony with God.

**The Way of
Healing.** And you cannot deal with your sin, you cannot put it away. You may mourn over it on the one hand, though the old hymn is true: 'Weeping will not save me;' or you may make light of it on the other. You may try to forget your complaint and lay aside your sorrow, and comfort yourself; but it is not dealt with thus; the sore remains. It is the man reconciled to *God*, whose sin *He* puts away, whom *He* lifts up, and he alone, who is healed. That man should face God feeling His reality, His holiness, His grace, face Him and submit to Him, is the great and vital need.

'Speak not one against another' (ver. 11). There seems to be little or no connection between this paragraph and the one we have just been considering. The apostle seems to be harping upon the old string, *the sins of the tongue*,

98

A Danger and a Remedy

and bringing in once more the warning which he cannot keep out of his exhortations to his Christian countrymen. But I suggest that there may be a subtle connection between the two paragraphs.

James iv. II, I2.

Is it not true that when your conscience begins to prick and accuse you for your faults, you are disposed to soothe its wounds with the plaister of your neighbours' failings ? Is it not true that the tongues that most glibly and volubly descant upon the failings of Christian people belong to the least spiritually-minded ? Is there not some relief to a conscience ill at ease in plunging into a consideration of the vices and shortcomings of other people ? It is a convenient refuge into which to run from the inexorable demands of conscience. And this passage asks that a man shall deal severely with himself first of all, for until he has dealt with himself he is not fit to deal with anybody else. It intimates pretty plainly that we are only adding another to the sum of our transgressions, and violating the law of brotherly love, when we sit in judgment on one another in the house of God ; and it seems to suggest that if a man will come face to face with the ' One only law-giver, who is able to save and destroy,' if only he will stand for a moment consciously in the august presence of the Holiest,

A Subtle Temptation.

The General Epistle of James

James iv. 11, 12. and see his own foulness in that moment, and realise the power that has spared him when it might have destroyed him, he will have little inclination left to speak evil of his brother or to judge his neighbour.

I am not suggesting that we should never express any opinion upon our neighbours' actions, that however wrong he is we should never speak disparagingly of him. It is better generally to speak *to* him than *of* him, and it requires more **A Call to Self-Scouting.** Christian courage. What is suggested strongly is that we should deal with ourselves in the presence of God before we deal with our neighbours, and that our dealing with our neighbour should be carried out in a spirit of humble submission to God, and not of pharisaic superiority. Everywhere God resisteth the proud, and it is not my business to adjudicate on the question as to who is a true Christian and who is not. My chief business is to live near to God myself, and with loving and lowly earnestness to seek to bring others into the same nearness that I enjoy.

XX

PLANNING WITHOUT GOD

JAMES iv. 13, 14

Go to now, ye that say, To-day or to-morrow we will go into this city, and spend a year there, and trade, and get gain: whereas ye know not what shall be on the morrow. What is your life? For ye are a vapour, that appeareth for a little time, and then vanisheth away.

THIS paragraph, reaching to the end of ch. iv., suggests submission to the will of God in view of the helplessness and uncertainty of human life. It is not certain that in it and the next James is speaking distinctly to Christian people; you notice that he does not call them 'brethren.' For my own part I think he is not, but that he is speaking to Jews, and therefore to people who profess to fear God. He makes us see the busy, bustling trader, his head full of schemes and plans for business, who puts his finger on the map and indicates a city and unfolds his plans. He is going to start out to-morrow, and he is going to stay at the city a year, to trade and to make money.

James iv. 13, 14. The Busy Man.

101

The General Epistle of James

James iv. 13, 14. A Serious Omission. It is not wrong to travel and trade and make gain; the world could not hang together but for the enterprise of such men as these. What is foolish and wrong is, that the man is speaking as if he were absolute lord of to-morrow, and next year, and his faculties for making gain. The portrait is drawn of the pushing, eager man of the world, who in all his buying and selling, plans and acts as though he were master of his own life, as though God had nothing to do with it, who ignores God, and never consults His will, never submits his plans to the Divine judgment, in whose consciousness God does not dwell. He may be an honest trader, an industrious and enterprising trader, he may be in touch with religious organisations. But the whole plan of his life is made apart from God, his whole business life is divorced from God, and as far as his affairs are concerned, God might not exist.

Planning without God. And James reminds this man, and all of us who read his letter to-day, that this is amazing folly. You know nothing about to-morrow. It may dawn for you, or it may not. If it does, you know not what it may discover to you, what failure of power, what presence of disease, reverse of fortune, change of circumstance, new perplexity. Here are the facts : 'You know not.'

102

Planning without God

You are as a vapour, an unsubstantial, unstable, uncertain element.

James iv. 13, 14.

There is a God who has a will for your life and your to-morrow. You may ask of Him, and receive from Him wisdom, guidance, illumination of judgment, strength of purpose. He has but to put forth His finger and touch your brain, your heart, and all your plans are overthrown; or again, He has only to touch your mountains of difficulty, and they vanish like vapour. His name is love, His will is good will. What unutterable folly and wrong to plan your life without reference and deference to Him! To be plunging hither and thither in the dim light of your own judgment, when you might be walking on the high firm road of His making and in the clear light of His approval.

The folly of ignoring His Power.

XXI

IF THE LORD WILL

JAMES iv. 15-17.

FOR that ye ought to say, If the Lord will, we shall both live, and do this or that. But now ye glory in your vauntings: all such glorying is evil. To him therefore that knoweth to do good, and doeth it not, to him it is sin.

James iv. 15-17. 'YE ought to say, If the Lord will.' That is the spirit in which you ought to live, reminding yourself every day—of what? The shortness of life? Yes, and the will of God, which is always good.

The Happiness of Realised Dependence. If the Lord will, we shall live—If the Lord will, we shall cease to live here, and shall live elsewhere. To say this will remind me of the power, the loving power that over-arches my whole life. I am not the sport of chance and accident. I am not a piece of driftwood on the stream of time. I am a child loved of the Father, who has His loving purpose for me; and the chief end of my life is to fulfil that purpose.

If I succeed, as people say, in my buying and

104

If the Lord Will

selling, or in my teaching or writing, or preaching, **James iv.** I shall be saved from evil boasting, from talking **15-17.** of my skill or my industry, or of the good luck which has not deserted me.

And if I fall on evil times, using men's language again, I shall neither be envious nor despairing. I am being led, and I shall have that which is sweeter than all earthly good—the consciousness that I am fulfilling the will of God. 'Though I walk through the valley of the shadow of death, I will fear no evil, for Thou art with me.'

If the Lord will that I should go up or down, He will give me the needed strength to do either. I believe that He may will a dark experience for me of trial and strain, of loss and disappointment. But I believe that He can turn the valley of weeping into a place of springs, and can help me to do so by His grace.

Here is what we *ought* to say, according to **The Lord** our passage : 'If the Lord will'—not of necessity **shall decide for me.** to write in it every letter, or to say it in so many words; but to write it deeply on our hearts, and to have it always before us. 'If the Lord will,' I shall go here or there, to this work or that pleasure, to this companionship or that alliance. If the Lord will *not*, I shall not go. I shall bear solitude, dishonour, reproach.

Let this be our resolve now ; it is not a high

105

The General Epistle of James

James iv. 15-17.

virtue, it is simple Christian duty. We ought to say, and we *know* we ought to say: 'If the Lord will,' and, according to the last verse of this chapter, 'To him that knoweth to do good, and doeth it not, to him it is sin.'

XXII

GREEDY RICH AND
SUFFERING POOR

JAMES v. 1-6

Go to now, ye rich, weep and howl for your miseries that are coming upon you. Your riches are corrupted, and your garments are moth-eaten. Your gold and your silver are rusted ; and their rust shall be for a testimony against you, and shall eat your flesh as fire. Ye have laid up your treasure in the last days. Behold, the hire of the labourers who mowed your fields, which is of you kept back by fraud, crieth out : and the cries of them that reaped have entered into the ears of the Lord of Sabaoth. Ye have lived delicately on the earth, and taken your pleasure ; ye have nourished your hearts in a day of slaughter. Ye have condemned, ye have killed the righteous *one* ; he doth not resist you.

WE have two distinct paragraphs in this passage ; **James v.** to use a phrase of the Old Testament prophets, two **1-6.** distinct 'Oracles of the Lord.' The former of the two is obviously not addressed to Christian people, the latter as obviously is. There is an entire absence of the term 'brethren' in the first six verses ; in the second six it occurs no fewer than four times. There is a most vigorous and fierce

The General Epistle of James

James v. 1-6. indictment in the first part, and nothing else; while in the second there is gentle and affectionate entreaty. The first is a storm of lightning and thunder and violent rain. The second is like the gentle dew and the blessed sunshine of a spring morning, coaxing the growth and development of all beautiful things.

The Offence of the Rich. We have noticed, in previous parts of the epistle, that the chief opposition to the Christians of this time came from the rich. They were persons who blasphemed the name of Christ, oppressed His followers, and dragged them into courts of justice. We have seen James' rebuke to those Christians who favoured the persons of the rich, and gave them the chief seats, and flattered them when they visited the Christian assemblies. Now we are to see how he pours out upon them the vials of his wrath and indignation, and why. And we must make up our minds as to the way in which we regard this scathing passage—whether merely as the outpouring of the scorn of an austere ascetic on the vices of the rich, vices into which the Christians were in danger of falling, or as the utterance and writing of a man inspired of the Holy Ghost. The former is the rationalist's way; the latter is the true way of the man who believes that these writings are not mere human opinions and

Greedy Rich and Suffering Poor

judgments, but the utterances of men who spake as they were moved by the Holy Ghost. For my own part I listen to these paragraphs as to the words of a prophet inspired of God.

James v. 1-6.

At the very outset we observe that James speaks of miseries that are about to fall upon the rich, and he bids them weep and howl. What were the miseries? In all probability those connected with the destruction of Jerusalem foretold by our Lord, and so mingled in His teaching with His own second advent as to be practically inextricable. As one of the old prophets, Habakkuk, for example, mounts his watch-tower and sees the coming of the Chaldean scourge sweeping over the land of Judah and the city of Jerusalem and foretells it, calling it the judgment of the Lord, so James feels in his soul the solemnity of the impending judgment on the Holy City, in which the wealthier Jews were robbed of everything; a judgment succeeded by a reign of terror, which prevailed wherever Jews were found. So verse 3 reads, ' Ye have *heaped treasure together for the last days,*' and verse 5 : ' *Ye have pampered your hearts in a day of slaughter.*' The metaphor is roughly that of a beast who is unconsciously fattening himself for the shambles. So these

Sorrows to Come.

109

The General Epistle of James

James v. 1-6. people are hoarding their money for the spoiler to seize. They will simply be the richer prey for him because of the treasure which they are heaping together. So in an external sense their wealth is their undoing; they will be the first to be seized upon in the reign of terror. And inasmuch as they have lived exclusively for this, their hearts will be torn and rent when all they have is taken from them, or they are taken from it.

That is not all. Therein lay their folly, but **Sin, as well as Folly.** beneath the folly lay the sin, and it is the sin that James denounces. We see clearly what the sin is, the love of money which our Lord denounced, and which St Paul declared to be the root of all evil. You see what these people are doing, heaping treasure together, laying it up in what they consider safe places, that they may make a show with it. You see how they are living (verse 5)— luxuriously, extravagantly; instead of keeping down their wants to the lowest minimum, increasing them, inventing new ways of self-indulgence.

The Dangers of Wealth It is the inveterate tendency of human nature; the possession of wealth tends to luxury, to take the life clear away from simplicity into self-indulgence, and self-indulgence invariably hardens and materialises the heart. Nobody is more selfish, more brutally callous to the claims, needs,

110

Greedy Rich and Suffering Poor

and sufferings of others than the self-indulgent man. What you see in this paragraph by the vivid light of St James' rhetoric is tarnished money, corrupted money, laid up by a man from selfish motives, that he may have more to spend upon luxuries and show, and not that he may have wherewith to provide for need in a dark and troubled day. He is heaping it up and exulting in his heart at the thought of what he has.

James v. 1-6.

Further, in order that he may accumulate the more, *he is defrauding the labourer in the matter of his wages.* Either because wealth gives him power and that he may have the more for his luxuries, paying far less than he ought to his working man, or keeping him waiting for his wages after his work is done, absolutely indifferent to his needs. So the poor agricultural labourer, ever a pathetic figure, underpaid, despised, oppressed, is brought into the picture. And further still, these people are represented—it is another characteristic of the hardening effect of the love of money—as hating those who are just and right, those who protest against their method of life, and sweeping them out of their path. 'Ye have condemned; ye have killed the just; he doth not resist you.' It reminds one of the charge of Stephen (Acts vii. 51, 52): 'Ye stiffnecked

—And its Sins.

111

The General Epistle of James

James v.
1-6.

and uncircumcised in heart and ears, ye do always resist the Holy Ghost; as your fathers did, so do ye. Which of the prophets have not your fathers persecuted? and they have slain them which showed before of the coming of the Just One; of whom ye have been now the betrayers and murderers.' Whether James is referring here to just people who have been done to death by his countrymen, or to Him who was pre-eminently the Just One, is not certain, *but he might well be foretelling his own death.* He was called 'the Just,' and was stoned and clubbed to death in the streets of Jerusalem. It is a terrible charge to bring against people, and shows clearly the effect of worldly indulgence upon the character, by making it perfectly selfish and pitiless.

And the
Nemesis.

There is another side to this. James seems to say, there is no safe place for wealth, as represented by precious metals or costly garments; it gets eaten into and decays. Here are men who have succeeded in getting their own way. Their workers are in their power, and they have defrauded them of their rights. They have swept out of the way the protests of the just, silencing all remonstrance. They have gathered in their hoard and are exulting in their skill. And they do not know that they are securing their own undoing and condemnation; that the

Greedy Rich and Suffering Poor

rust and decay going on in their possessions is **James v.** but a symbol of that which is going on in their **1-6.** own natures. That, like a moth in the costly fabric of a garment, and rust in precious metal, all that is good and noble and worthy is being eaten out of their natures by this accursed spirit of worldliness which they are cherishing. And it is ever true; love of money, love of pleasure, love of display, will eat away all your fine Christian enthusiasm, all your care for others, all your interest in spiritual things, will make you absolutely useless, will defeat the purpose of God for you, and bring you under His condemnation at last.

There is yet another aspect. The cry of the helpless agricultural labourer, ay, and the cry of the underpaid seamstress, the cry of the poor worker kept waiting for his hire by the whim or caprice or the greed of the thoughtless or selfish employer, comes into the ears of the Lord of hosts. **The Lord** If it means anything at all, it means that God is **Sees.** on the side of the oppressed and wronged. That there is not a tragedy of want and work being enacted anywhere to-day, but He regards it. And there is a terrible reckoning awaiting the man who has oppressed the hireling in his wages. This apostle is at one with all the great Bible-writers in declaring that the cry of the wronged

H   113

The General Epistle of James

**James v.
1-6.**

is not unheard, you can shut it out of your ears,
it enters into the ears of the Lord of hosts, and
in the terrific words of the former part of this
epistle : 'He shall have judgment without mercy,
who hath showed no mercy.'

XXIII

A PLEA FOR PATIENCE

JAMES v. 7-12

BE patient therefore, brethren, until the coming of the Lord. Behold, the husbandman waiteth for the precious fruit of the earth, being patient over it, until it receive the early and latter rain. Be ye also patient; stablish your hearts: for the coming of the Lord is at hand. Murmur not, brethren, one against another, that ye be not judged; behold, the judge standeth before the doors. Take, brethren, for an example of suffering and of patience, the prophets who spake in the name of the Lord. Behold, we call them blessed which endured: ye have heard of the patience of Job, and have seen the end of the Lord, how that the Lord is full of pity, and merciful. But above all things, my brethren, swear not, neither by the heaven, nor by the earth, nor by any other oath: but let your yea be yea, and your nay, nay; that ye fall not under judgement.

WE turn from the oppressor to the oppressed; at any rate, from the man who is living for this world, and whose soul is being surely destroyed, to the people who are suffering for the truth's sake, and are perhaps disposed to break out into envy of their more fortunate neighbours, or are in danger of breaking down through pressure of trial. And the paragraph resolves itself into an

James v. 7-12.

115

The General Epistle of James

James v. 7-12. affectionate appeal to stedfast endurance. The word translated, 'patience,' means more than it says. It is not the word originally so translated, that is used in connection with Job in verse 11. The literal meaning of the word in verse 7 is 'long-tempered,' the temper that can endure provocation, disappointment, which is not turned back by threatening or difficulty, malicious opposition, or even persecution.

Advice to the Tempted. The Jewish Christians were under immense pressure to be envious of the prosperity of their fellow-countrymen, who hated their faith; to tone down their zeal, to be untrue, to turn away from Christ, and this is a call to renewed patience. 'Do not grow reckless, nor hopeless,' he seems to say, 'nor violent: endure.' Do not let repining words escape you against people who suffer less than you (verse 9). Do not give way to violent speech, as oaths and curses, which I take to be the meaning of verse 12. Endure all the blows that fall upon you for Christ's sake with a calm and stedfast heart, under provocation and reviling and wronging. Be long-suffering.

Hard but necessary Counsel. Now this is hard counsel to follow, and there are people who need the counsel to-day, people whose high purpose is sorely tried, who are terribly provoked and greatly perplexed, who are in a minority in their place of business and their

116

A Plea for Patience

home; and who would say to-day: ' It is very **James v.** hard to be patient, with so much going on about **7-12.** you that is un-Christian and anti-Christian,' who sometimes wonder why God permits people to be so sorely tried. There are some to whom this word comes at this very moment, it may be, who seem to themselves to have come to the farthest verge of endurance, and are on the point of giving all up.

Now observe, this counsel does not stand by itself. The apostle enforces it and reinforces it with illustration and with doctrine. He recognises, as the whole Bible does, how hard it is to be patient. If it were not so hard, if there were not so many provocations, misunderstandings, annoyances, difficulties, so much would not be said about it.

So he just brings illustrations to strengthen **Examples of** his appeal. He points to the farmer who tills his **Patience.** land, and sows his seed, and then, through all trials of climate, and they are many, waits patiently, expecting a harvest. He points to the prophets, as to men who have to stand alone, to walk a solitary path, to suffer evil. The noble men, the men who spoke in the name of the Lord, had often to live in a perfect storm of persecution; and their fidelity, their persistent endurance, should hearten every tried soul. He speaks of

117

The General Epistle of James

James v. 7-12. Job, and uses another and common word for patience, desirous, apparently, of showing that God may permit men to be severely tried, and yet not suffer them to be beaten. He may be exceedingly pitiful, and full of tender mercy towards them while they are under the trial. You will observe that not a word is said about the pity of the Lord or His tender mercy in the previous paragraph addressed to the rich.

One wonders why in this connexion James does not mention the endurance of his Divine Kinsman, the supreme example of long-suffering, as the writer of the Hebrews does. It is one of the defects of his letter.

The Blessing of Trial. The great doctrine is that *God is very near to the tried Soul:* and Christian people who have experienced it would tell you that it is worth while enduring trial a hundred times over, to be made conscious of the actual nearness and tender personal love of God. It is an experience which the man who will not face trial, who will not bear it for Christ's sake, can never know.

The Promise of the Coming. The other great doctrine, intended to enforce the courage and patience of these Jewish Christians, is that of the COMING OF THE LORD. The Parousia, the arrival, the presence of the Lord *' draweth nigh.'* It is quite clear that the early Christians expected that in their time the Lord

118

A Plea for Patience

Jesus would visibly appear in the glory of His Father; that the heaven would suddenly glow with splendour; that Christ would be seen seated on His throne; that the dead would be raised from their graves; and that over those Christians who remained a great and wonderful change would pass, and they would be gathered to their eternal home. St Paul taught that in his earliest letters, and it is significant that in his last letters, notably those to the Philippians and Timothy, that teaching finds no place; but that he speaks of going to be with Christ, and of a day when the Lord, the righteous Judge, shall give him the crown of righteousness. Dr Dale, in one of his last sermons, suggests that the two things may be one—that the moment of Paul's departing to be with Christ may be also the moment of Christ's glorious coming to the soul of His servant. We cannot tell. We do know that there was no further visible appearing of the Lord in Paul's day, or that of James, and that to this extent the expectations of the early Christians were unrealised.

James v. 7-12.

The day of the Lord may be a day that lasts through thousands of years, and even thousands of generations. It may be that He comes again to each generation of Christian people as they pass hence into the realities of the unseen world.

An Event Deferred yet Certain.

119

The General Epistle of James

James v. 7-12. We may be sure that He comes to receive the soul of each true disciple of His as it quits the tabernacle of its earthly house, and that at the last, when the course of humanity is run, the great saying of Paul will be fulfilled, that those who are alive and remain will be caught up to meet the Lord in glory.

We are in the presence of a great mystery, and the fanciful imagination of the literalist has sometimes made the solemn subject grotesque, while time and strength have been wasted in profitless speculations as to the time of an event which is hidden from all men, and even from the angels in heaven.

Face to Face with God—some day. This is certain : that every one of us must come face to face with God, and that at any moment the summons to meet Him may come. The accompaniments are of small importance, whether through awe-inspiring manifestations, or through the experiences of a sick-chamber, or through some tragic happening. However it may be, the soul must stand face to face with Christ. And, in that moment of epiphany to the faithful and chosen soul, wounds will be healed, wrongs will be righted, sorrows and strain will be ended, and the eternal peace will have come.

And now, the Lord is here. Meanwhile let one sentence in this paragraph be written on our hearts to-day, 'The Judge

A Plea for Patience

standeth before the doors.' *The Lord is here,* James v. 7-12. and He is watching thy life and judging it now, seeing and hearing, searching and sifting. I know nothing more solemnising than that; not even the fact that He shall come again and His fuller glory shall break on human vision. He is here, and He knows thy heart, whether thou lovest Him and art faithful to Him, or no. Whether thou carest for the things for which His heart is set, or only for the things for which the world cares. Oh! that thou wouldest listen to His voice, and become aware of His presence. For thy Judge is thy Redeemer and thy best Friend.

XXIV

PRAYER AND MEANS

JAMES v. 13-15

Is any among you suffering? let him pray. Is any cheerful? let him sing praise. Is any among you sick? let him call for the elders of the Church; and let them pray over him, anointing him with oil in the name of the Lord: and the prayer of faith shall save him that is sick, and the Lord shall raise him up; and if he have committed sins, it shall be forgiven him.

James v. 13-15. The Power of Prayer. WE come in this closing paragraph upon one of the characteristic notes of this epistle. All the way through it has insisted on the necessity and the extreme value of prayer. '*Let him ask of God who giveth*' is one of its earliest notes, now 'Let him *pray*,' 'Let him call for the elders of the Church, and let them *pray*.' '*Pray* one for another.' 'Elijah, your great saint and hero, was a man of prayer.' 'The supplication of a righteous man availeth much in its working.' 'The prayer of faith shall save the sick.' James has no philosophy of prayer to offer, but he remembered the prayers of his Divine Brother, and in the habit of prayer he had followed Him. The tradition

Prayer and Means

concerning James is that his knees were worn **James v. 13-15.** hard as a camel's through his constant habit of prayer. All his strength he had derived from fellowship with the Highest in prayer.

He is writing to Christian people, and he is **The Resort in Suffering.** saying in greater detail what Paul urged later on, 'In everything by prayer and supplication with thanksgiving let your requests be made known to God.' So he begins, 'Is any among you suffering?' (*literally*, 'suffering evil') 'let him pray.' He may feel constrained to do other things, to try to remove the evil, to secure brotherly love and sympathy in the suffering. But whatever he does or does not do, 'let him pray'; there is help and comfort there, close at hand. And prayer may save him from many things — from folly, from breaking down in patience and courage and faithfulness; from whining and complaining and bitterness of spirit, from sullenness and from terror. Prayer pierces through appearances to the reality of God, draws His presence about the soul, calms and strengthens the weary and tried heart.

When a man is suffering, he is tempted to **The Comfort of Prayer.** forgo prayer. Then let him fight the temptation and persist in the endeavour. The whole consensus of Christian experience goes to prove that in the shadow of His wings there is safety,

123

The General Epistle of James

James v. 13-15. rest and peace. At this very moment, with your eye on this word, you may be suffering evil. You are wondering how you can bear the evil, or by what means you can remove it. Look once more at this injunction, and be assured of its supreme importance. God comes nearer to His own in the day when they are suffering evil wrongfully for His sake than at any other time. We know of whom it is written, 'Being in an agony, He prayed—as He prayed the fashion of His countenance was changed.'

The Expression of Joy. '*Is any merry (cheerful), let him sing praise.*' We must contrast this for a moment with *verse* 9 of the previous chapter. There are times when joy needs to be suppressed, when it is false; that is, when the heart is out of harmony with God, and alienated from Him. But there

—In Song. are also times when it must be allowed to have its vent, and here is the natural vent, '*Let him sing.*' The literal meaning of the word rendered 'merry' in the Authorised Version, and 'cheerful' in the Revised Version is 'well in mind.' Is any one thus—with all the flow of spirits which belong to it? let him sing, but let him sing praise. Let him remember God in his gladness. Do not let him suffer his boisterous spirits to carry him away from God. Sing, but sing praise. You may sometimes sing away an evil mood.

124

Prayer and Means

Law, in his *Serious Call*, speaking of that **James v.** nourishment of the soul by private devotion **13-15.** which every Christian needs, and which he neglects at his peril, urges strongly that song should find a place in it, as well as reading and prayer. It is very important; we were made to sing. Next to teaching our children the Scriptures, we can do them no greater service, in view of the after struggles of life, than putting into their lips and memories songs of praise to God. Nothing exalts the soul more than songs of praise. They offer a very wide and varied field for the mind to traverse. Of Nature, and all its wonders and glories, of human love, with all its bliss, of friendship, of hearth and home, of native land, and of all sacred and beautiful things, the soul may pour forth its song of praise to God. Here is the lesson of the two opening sentences. In the gloomy valley and the sunny height, in the dark hour of pain and woe, and in every dream of earthly bliss, let the heart turn to God. You will observe that, from verse 14 onwards, **Fellowship** James goes on to teach that there should be **and Service.** fellowship both in prayer and praise, both in gloom and gladness, that the Christian heart should not seek to live in solitude. These verses are most important in their bearing on the life of a Christian Church, and the great outstanding

The General Epistle of James

James v. 13-15. lesson is that there is to be the closest possible friendship of sympathy amongst members.

The elders of the Church were to hold themselves in readiness to serve any member of the Church at any time with prayer and sympathy and spiritual counsel. It is evident that there were a number of such men in each separate Church. They were expected to be men who could offer the prayer of faith, and who would respond when they were called upon to visit cases of sickness and trouble. It is a side of Christian fellowship that needs to be developed. The elders of a Church have peculiar responsibility for the members of the Church. 'Feed the Church of God,' said St Paul to the elders of the Ephesian Church, 'which He hath purchased with His own blood.'

The Appeal to the Elders. There is one point which must not be overlooked in this connexion. Let the sick man *call for* the elders of the Church. There is not a man among the elders who would refuse to come if he were called for; let the sick person send a message to the elders or to the presiding elder, the minister. Do not let him wait to see if the elders or the minister will discover by some special illumination or intuition that he is sick. Do not let him lie and complain in his solitary trouble that he is slighted and neglected, and

Prayer and Means

that no one cares. Let him *call for* the elders **James v. 13-15.** of the Church ; he has a right to their sympathy, let him exert his right, and claim the sympathy.

The instructions as to how the elders shall act **The Ministry to the Sick.** in the presence of the sick are not altogether free from difficulty. One thing is perfectly clear, they are to pray, to unite in prayer with the sick person himself. 'Anointing with oil in the name of the Lord' appears to have been practised here and there after the age in which James wrote ; and in time it became, not a rite followed in the hope of restoring health, but rather a preparation for death. And so in the twelfth century it came to be called the Last or Extreme Unction. The Roman catechism says it is not to be performed unless the person is dangerously ill ; and it is to be efficacious in the remission of sins and the comfort of the dying. This, however, St James never intended, for he says, 'the prayer of faith shall save the sick, and the Lord shall raise him up.' You will observe that it is the prayer of faith that is the power for the sick man, both healing of body and soul—there is probably a subtle connection between the sickness and sin in verse 15.

It would be interesting to discuss the bearing **Prayer and Means.** of this verse on the present time. Always let it be remembered that the use of means is recommended in the anointing, which is not a mere

127

The General Epistle of James

James v. 13-15. sacred charm ; also that the gift of healing, as the gift of tongues, was a part of the original endowment of the Christian Church ; that this gift was used very sparingly ; that Paul laboured with a life-long malady ; that he left Trophimus at Miletus sick ; that good people undoubtedly died in apostolic times. There would be, I suppose, cases in which the elders would feel that they could not offer the prayer of faith. The Spirit of God, which forbade Paul to preach the word in Asia, working upon these men, would forbid the prayer, because the will of God would be, that now the earthly course should terminate, or that the sickness of body should remain for the cleansing and ennoblement of the soul and for the blessing of others.

Answered Prayers. For the rest, the injunction retains all its ancient force for present times. The prayers of a Christian community have been answered again and again in the raising from the very gates of the grave those for whom prayers have been offered. We need not go far to seek cases among our own beloved friends, concerning whose raising up reverence and awe have fallen upon our souls, as we have said, ' This is an answer to prayer.' We cried to God, He sent us light, He gave skill to the physician and surgeon, and by His blessing healing has come. The art of healing has

Prayer and Means

wondrously developed since the days of James. James v. Lives are saved by thousands now, that would 13-15. have been sacrificed then. There is no more precious gift of God to men than a Christian doctor. Christian people should use the art of healing, and believe in the art of prayer.

There is a reference to healing in verse 16, which is not to be overlooked. Confess your sins, 'therefore' (do not leave out the conjunction, it connects verses 15 and 16), 'one to another, that ye may be healed.' Does that mean physically? It is quite possible. Every one knows that often the chief hindrance to recovery, and even the chief cause of sickness, is that 'something on the mind,' which a wise doctor will discover in diagnosing his case. And we all have heard equally often of the rapid recovery when the burden has been lifted from the soul. It is not without instruction that our Lord's first word to the paralytic is : 'Thy sins are forgiven.' Unhappy relations between husband and wife, parent and child, minister and people, involve a severe strain on the energies of nerve and body.

Inter-dependence of Body and Mind.

XXV

THE MINISTRY OF RESTORATION

JAMES v. 16-20

CONFESS therefore your sins one to another, and pray one for another, that ye may be healed. The supplication of a righteous man availeth much in its working. Elijah was a man of like passions with us, and he prayed fervently that it might not rain ; and it rained not on the earth for three years and six months. And he prayed again ; and the heaven gave rain, and the earth brought forth her fruit. My brethren, if any among you do err from the truth, and one convert him ; let him know, that he which converteth a sinner from the error of his way shall save a soul from death, and shall cover a multitude of sins.

James v. 16-20. Mutual Confession. THERE is more than appears in the counsel, 'Confess your sins one to another, and pray one for another.' You might, perhaps, set some heart leaping with health and gladness to-day by obeying your part of this injunction. People wear their hearts out in estrangements ; friction is created by that native stubbornness in defending a fault rather than confess it, which is too

The Ministry of Restoration

characteristic of us all. We are perpetually James v. inclined to dwell on the faults of others, to the 16-20. entire neglect of our own. Now, 'confess,' not to a priest, but to one another. Fix your eyes on your own fault and confess it, not to God merely, but to the person against whom it was committed, and probably he will follow suit, and kneeling together in confession to the same Lord you may begin a new life.

The injunction sheds important light on The Worth Christian friendships. One of its chief uses is of Confession. confession. I am a most hearty believer in confession. One of the great needs of my life is a sympathetic human ear, into which I can tell the failings and defeats, the weakness and sin of my life, and whose confidence I can receive back again, whose prayers will mingle with mine in a passionate desire for a purer and holier life. To an official as such I cannot confess, and such a thing was never intended. To a sympathetic Christian heart I will, and through that heart God will send me peace and help.

Here is the great burden of this passage to Fellowship, Christian hearts: Do not seek to live to your- not Isolation. selves. There is no chance for you that way. Live in fellowship with God by prayer, and in fellowship with men by sympathy. And above all, believe in the efficacy of prayer. Do not think

131

The General Epistle of James

James v. 16-20. that it is merely the prerogative of a few princely souls. Elijah became what he was, and wielded the power which he did, through prayer. There is no record in the Old Testament of Elijah praying that it might not rain, he appears before Ahab suddenly with the prophecy that rain shall not come. And though he prays on Mount Carmel, it is after the message, 'Go show thyself to Ahab, and I will send rain.' He, worshipped of the Jew, beyond any other prophet, was a man of like passions with us. You simply do not know, James seems to say, what power you have in your hands in the exercise of prayer, nor what God will do for the soul that lives in communion with Him. 'He is able to do exceeding abundantly above all that we ask or think.'

The Church out of which prayer is gone will be an impotent Church, and the Christian who has lost the holy art of prayer will be a Christian entirely lacking spiritual power.

The Dangers of Over-Confidence. The last two verses of the epistle open up to us possibilities of at once the most solemn and blessed character. Think first of the solemn possibility. A Christian may err from the truth. James has pointed out the peril of the way. A Christian man may be led astray from the high road of faith and goodness, through his own

132

The Ministry of Restoration

strong passion, by his own lust, by the love of the **James v. 16-20.** world, he may be enticed. His taste for spiritual pleasures may be vitiated and his desire for them destroyed. He may be led so far astray as to need a second conversion. He may go so far wrong as to be in danger of death, the death of the soul. *There* is the tocsin of alarm, which Paul unites with James, and both with their Lord in sounding out to over-secure souls. And it is never needless. You can neglect the culture of your spiritual life, you can trifle and toy with unspiritual pleasures until you are face to face with spiritual ruin and death.

That is the first possibility to be laid to heart by all Christian people, and the very thought of it should lead us to labour with all diligence to make our calling and election sure.

The second is the possibility of restoration, and **The Ministry of Reconciliation.** all the blessed results that follow it. The erring brother may be restored, and that through human agency. Observe that this great responsibility and privilege is thrown upon the shoulders of the whole community. It is not said: 'If any of you do err from the truth, let the elders be called for.' The blessed ministry of reconciliation, of restoring harmony between the soul and its Lord, a ministry that angels might covet, is open to the simplest and lowliest Christian. Do you know

The General Epistle of James

James v. 16-20.

anybody who is erring from the truth to-day being caught away by the world, by temptation, by appetite? Do not say it is no business of yours, and do not on the other hand go about denouncing him. Do not shun and scorn him: '*Pray* for him that he may be healed,' and for yourself, that you may know how to act, and then set to work to try to turn him again. He is in a worse plight than the sick man for whom you are concerned. He is in danger of a worse than any physical death, and you may be the chosen instrument—think of it—to lead him back to the truth of God. It will involve trouble and pains, and heart-ache on your part, but it is the most blessed work in this world or in any other. When the prodigal is restored, and the arches of heaven ring with the joy of his return, you will know that it was through you that he came back to the shelter and bliss of the Father's house. Think of it again, the simplest Christian may win the eternal gratitude of God and of the soul that was turned again to Him, because through his wise and loving persistency the lost jewel was recovered, and the child of God's love, for whom Christ died, was brought home.

The letter ends very abruptly. There is no leave-taking. It could not close with a more

The Ministry of Restoration

impressive note. May that note sound in our **James v.** hearts to-day and continually, until it becomes a **16-20.** real part of the business of our lives to help our dear Lord in His shepherdly work of restoring the erring, and saving souls from death, and ensuring through our loving labour their cleansing from sin.

THE END.

Printed in the USA
CPSIA information can be obtained
at www.ICGtesting.com
LVHW020711061023
760082LV00012B/15